THE ORGANIZED SONGWRITER

HOW TO CREATE SPACE TO WRITE YOUR BEST SONGS

SIMON HAWKINS

Great
British
Book
Publishing

GET YOUR FREE WORKBOOK!

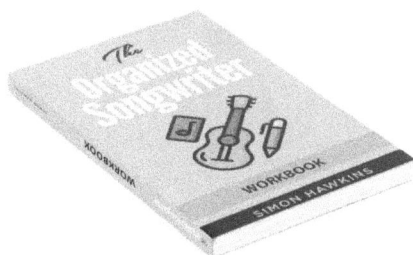

I've found that readers have the most success implementing the strategies in *The Organized Songwriter* when they have the opportunity to work through some real-life exercises and examples so they can put the principles in this book into practice.

To that end, to say thank you for purchasing this book, I'd like to give you the companion workbook for FREE!

Click at: http://bit.ly/orgwb.

To my beautiful, super-talented wife, Sandra.

To my inspiring children, Poppy, Monty, and Barty.

To Mum. Amazing.

To John F Smith, 1934 - 2020, friend, mentor.

To God, Author of all.

To all who carry a deep hunger to excel in their craft.

CONTENTS

INTRODUCTION

"Nothing is undoable. Just things not done."

INTRO

Time is short. Ridiculously short. As songwriters, there are a million things that try to take us away from our precious time doing what we love doing — the beautiful craft of songwriting. Whether we realize it or not, many songwriters have this problem: Not enough time and space.

Do any of these scenarios sound familiar?

- You try to sit down to write a cool song, but there are a million other things happening around you — family, friends, the dog, and a million other important things that need doing. Somehow you never seem to have the chance to do your best work as a songwriter.
- You are an incredibly creative person, awash in a sea of paperwork filled with great songs. But you're drowning. And when you need your best ideas, they are lost.
- You want to be a prolific songwriter but, just when you get the inspiration to write, there's not enough time to finish anything.

- You have plenty of ideas, but you're lost when it comes to picking the right tools to write like a pro.
- You have lots of material to take into a co-write, but when you look for a specific idea or lyric in your hook book, you just can't find it. The opportunity to write your best ideas is lost.
- You worry that life is moving way too fast for you to make an impact as a songwriter.

If any of these describe you, you're in good company! Virtually every songwriter I've ever worked with has struggled with at least one of these issues, and every successful songwriter has overcome these obstacles. If you're looking to step up your songwriting by beating these problems, there is one thing you'll need to do: get organized!

In *The Organized Songwriter — How to Create Space to Write Your Best Songs*, I give you a series of solutions to these issues. This book is filled with well-developed professional processes to keep track of your precious ideas that develop into completed songs. I also provide options for organizing professional tools of the trade as a songwriter as well as ways to prepare yourself to be the best co-writer you can be. And I'll reveal a second secret weapon and more.

Whether you've only just discovered the craft of songwriting or you're an experienced songwriter, this book contains insights into how you can become a more productive songwriter. By the end of the book, you'll be able to write like a pro, even if you don't call yourself a pro. As one of my heroes once said,

---

"Success occurs when opportunity meets preparation."

ZIG ZIGLAR

As songwriters, to make the most of whatever opportunities come to us, we need to be as prepared for it as best we can. That's what this book is all about.

While there are a million books about organizing your work, nothing contains new information exclusively for songwriters like this book.

I enjoyed building a foundation of knowledge about the craft from songwriting programs at Berklee College of Music and other sources, but I actually discovered the material for this book afterwards, from my experience as a professional songwriter, writing both on my own and in the writing rooms of Nashville. I actually became a songwriter after several years of working in the corporate world, and I learned firsthand that there are many tricks to organizing yourself as a song-writer that are not just helpful but essential to get signed. I've compiled those tricks into this book, so other songwriters can get a jump-start on what I only learned after years of struggle and guesswork.

This book is for songwriters who have lost opportunities because their best ideas have just not been there when they needed them. Or maybe those who have a million great song ideas, but somehow they just haven't been there when they were writing, either on their own or with a co-writer. This book is also for those who may be too creative to naturally organize themselves like a pro and are conse-quently missing the best of their songwriting career.

By the time you've finished reading The Organized Songwriter, you will be able to:

- Discover your own songwriter's mindset, your own 'why' to write, the way practice changes everything for the world's most successful writers, the importance of the idea of competencies, and the formula for getting songs cut.
- Understand the idea of the Song Chain and why it's incredibly important to be organized as a songwriter, as well

as an essential tool in my own tool kit: the Idea Bank. You'll learn how to capture fresh ideas, how to turn them into writable ideas, what to do with your best ideas to turn them into finished songs, how to know when a song is finished, and what is needed at each stage.

- Know how to be creative and prolific as a songwriter, even when you don't feel like it.
- Know how to organize your creative space and writing time like a pro, and how to make the most of your creative habits and education.
- Turn up confident to your co-writes, to best serve your co-writers to write the best song ever.
- Recognize the best way to put it all together, applying a similar approach to what successful people use in the corporate world.

In short, having put in place the ideas in this book, you will be an organized songwriter. You will be able to leverage your ideas, tools, and co-writing to enable you to be the best songwriter you can be. Because you deserve it.

As a staff songwriter at Universal Music Publishing in Nashville, I've been nominated for and won awards for my songs including Grammys, Doves, and hymn-writing awards. After spending many years in both creative and corporate careers, I've had the privilege to teach the material in this book to hundreds of songwriters who have found it invaluable. Known by many as the guy who teaches how to be an organized songwriter, I've enjoyed introducing these ideas to many creative people who made meaningful changes to their workflows; as a result, enabling them to write their best songs, making the most of their time to be productive.

Having completed the lessons in this book, you will transform your workflow as a songwriter like a pro. Whether it's capturing amazing fresh song ideas, creating your own creative space and time to work as a songwriter, developing your own craft, networks, and technology, you will walk into your co-writes with confidence, knowing how to serve your co-writers with multiple, brilliant ideas they would LOVE to write. Ultimately, you will organize yourself like a pro, spending your time and energy using a workflow that will enable you to write your best potential and calling as a songwriter.

Andrea Stolpe, an instructor at Berklee Music School, multi-platinum recorded songwriter, artist, and author, says about this book:

> "A fantastic read that cuts to the heart of what it feels like to struggle and triumph as a creative. This book is a wealth of action steps to push through the invisible barrier that keeps many of us stuck. A fresh perspective that blends the mystery of creativity and the tangibility of results-driven music-making."
>
> ANDREA STOLPE

Let me put this a different way: how would you feel if you were missing your very best ideas at your fingertips just because you're not organized? How would you feel if you arrived at a co-write without all of your best ideas with you? Or even having NO great ideas with you at all? And how would you feel if your peers were moving further with their craft and leaving you behind?

So, what would you feel like if you knew your very best ideas were available — everything, everywhere for your writing?

Pat Pattison, author of Songwriting Without Boundaries and Professor of Lyric Writing and Poetry at Berklee College of Music, said:

"Even if you have massive talent, you can learn to do it better, and with more consistency. Great singers use vocal coaches. Even in their prime, they continue the search. Writing is like that too."

PAT PATTISON

And he's right — it's up to each one of us to do all we can to achieve our full potential as songwriters. This book shows you how to be a better, organized songwriter.

As a legendary speaker and author Tony Robbins said:

"Life is a gift, and it offers us the privilege, opportunity, and responsibility to give something back by becoming more."

TONY ROBBINS

Your craft as a songwriter deserves to be taken to the next level. Let this book help you transform your songwriting by applying the methods here as part of your workflow to take your songs to their ultimate potential. All you need to do is keep reading to learn the benefits of being organized and how to manage your songwriting workflow like a pro. Discover these techniques and help grow as a songwriter so you can pursue your ultimate calling.

Read on. Be productive. You'll be surprised how much more you will be able to achieve. Just like a pro.

Overview

Before we begin your new journey with your songwriting, let's take a look at what exactly we'll be covering. I've split this book into several parts:

- The **Introduction** (here!)
- The **Mindsets part** is all about passion, including what a professional songwriter actually is, the idea of the songwriters' competencies, and the three categories to approach all new jobs or careers.
- The **Ideas and Songs part** includes how to capture our ideas everywhere, strategies for writing and completing songs, critical data for keeping control of your work, and how you can progress from concept to completed songs.
- The **Tools of the Trade part** covers how to organize our tools for the trade, such as essential elements needed for pro songwriters and what 'nice to have' tools are out there.
- The **Co-writing part** is everything you need to serve your co-writers best, making sure all your ideas are available to you at the right time and in the right place.
- The **Next Steps part** is all about focusing on the next steps of your journey as songwriters, managing success, the Song Funnel, and how and why songs don't get cut.
- Finally, the **Appendices** contain bonus information about important resources to help you on your journey.

Song Maps

Want to know more about one of the critical tools mentioned in this book, Song Maps? You can find out more about this strategy in my book *Song Maps — A New System to Write Your Best Lyrics* and the accompanying workbook, *Song Maps Workbook.*

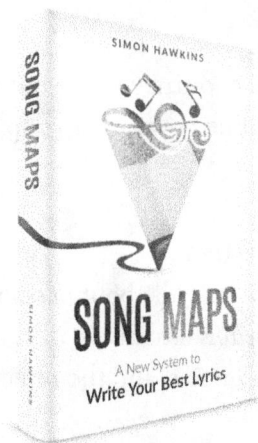

PART ONE
MINDSETS

"To be the best version of a songwriter I can be."

PASSION

Being creative is a beautiful part of life. It's not because it's easy or only just because it's fun. Being creative is mostly about doing hard work. So, if we are going to be doing any kind of work, especially creative work, we need to get our mindset right upfront.

Mindset is a set of assumptions, practices, or notions that create compelling reasons within ourselves to use certain behaviors, choices, and tools.

My aim here is to help you understand how pro songwriters behave — what drives them to become successful songwriters.

The fact you're reading this book means you are one of the creative individuals who are capable of producing successful songs. Here's the truth: you are creative. You are amazing, and you are a unique, incredible person. Now you need to learn what kind of mindset you need to turn those qualities into a successful songwriting career.

In this part of the book, I'm going to talk about:

- Different whys
- Passion
- Are you left or right-brained?
- What does a professional songwriter do?
- Competencies for songwriters
- Everything comes through practice
- The formula

Remember, part of being a pro songwriter is about being as obsessive about the process as you are about the craft. It's about making the journey with all the right stuff in your bag. It's about making sure you're getting to the right place at the right time.

But before you take that first step on your journey, or even start packing, you need to take the very important step of getting to know yourself. Suppose you know your why, you'll be able to pack and plan your songwriting path in a way that's right for you. Let's start getting to know you, so we know just what kind of songwriter matches your why. Let's get cracking!

Different Whys

Every songwriter has a *why* — a reason for writing songs and investing the kind of time, energy (both emotional and physical energy), intellectual work, and money in their creative pursuit. A songwriter may have one of several reasons for doing what they do. You could write songs:

1. For pleasure
2. For creative expression
3. For a hobby

4. For communities, worship, social events, fashion
5. For the money (commercial songwriting)

And there are probably a million other reasons to write songs. But, whatever it is, it's essential to figure out what that why is.

I have had the privilege of working with many different songwriters. Pro songwriters I co-write with, aspiring writers I teach, people I sit next to at award ceremonies, those who happen to be in my publisher's writing rooms, and some who are on my Worship Team. Every different songwriter has their own approach, journey, and reasons for being who they are and how they go about their work.

For me, writing songs is all about the three words that my life is about: God, love, and worship. I believe everyone is made with a God-given talent that should be used in whatever He would want us to do. Everyone has their own values and reasons, and of course, that's fine.

But for whatever reason you write, the trick is to establish the right mindset to enable you to become the best version of that songwriter you can be, whatever that looks like. And that starts with knowing your why.

So it's time to ask yourself: *why* do you want to write songs? It's OK if the answer doesn't come quickly or easily, but do take the time to have at least a somewhat plausible answer before moving on. After all, you can't begin your journey unless you know why you're going!

Passion

Once you have a good idea of your why as a songwriter, it's time to go a little deeper. Let's talk about what underlies that reason.

Everyone has their own passion for songwriting. For me, this passion has been with me since I was a child, mostly from growing up within the Church. The first-ever song I wrote is still in my paper files, and, to be honest, while it was a heartfelt song written from my faith in God, it wasn't very good at all. But no matter how good or bad an individual song may turn out to be, throughout my life, they have always been written with that passion, and that is what has carried me through my entire career.

This passion has been behind every step of my songwriting journey, starting with learning harmony, melody, and arrangements. A little later in life, it drove me to write lyrics, including rhyme, rhythm, structures, and the artistry behind combining both of these two journeys — music and lyrics — to enjoy this wonderful craft, songwriting.

Today, my passion for songwriting is still linked to my faith in God, rooted in the Bible.

"Whatever you do, work at it with all your heart, as working for the Lord, not for human masters."

COL 3:23

When I teach this session at Write About Jesus (WAJ), a workshop I've now taught for many years, many people have a similar reason for their passion for songwriting. And their passion is also to serve God with their work.

In other words, they have:

A passion to excel in serving God.

No matter where your passion comes from, you need to understand your passion. That passion will give you a reason to write, even through the hard times — if you don't already know, writing tends to involve work, discipline, time, and energy to make it all work, and passion is what will lead you through all that.

After I taught this session at WAJ, someone came up to me and said:

"Thanks **SO** much for this! I so need this because I have so many piles of paper around my house. I'm going to sort this out when I get home."

WAJ ATTENDEE

This writer had plenty of ideas and seemed to have no problem with the creative side of the process. However, their passion was being hampered as they realized their piles of paper meant that some of their best work was simply lost by not having a method to look after them. Sometimes, great ideas have been lost because they simply haven't come back at the right moment again. And for songwriters, this is tragic.

Not all creatives are naturally organized. Those without a mindset to organize their best work will be unheard, miss their chance, and become lost. And that's a shame. More than a shame, it's a disaster for them and everyone who could have heard their songs.

But wherever you find yourself on this journey, organizing your work as a songwriter is one of the most important things to do with your songwriting. It's the difference between your ideas being there with you, everything, everywhere, or left somewhere else, lost. It's the difference between investing in your craft or letting your passion be sabotaged by poor work habits. It's the difference between piles of paper everywhere and having everything you need right in your pocket. And we'll talk about this process and the Idea Bank more in Part 2.

ARE YOU LEFT OR RIGHT-BRAINED?

In case you aren't already familiar, neuroscience tells us that the brain's two hemispheres are set up for distinct varieties of tasks. Generally speaking, the left brain is responsible for language and logical thought, while the right brain controls visual and creative thinking.

Although these hemispheres are the same in most humans, it's an inescapable fact that everyone is wired differently. Some people are wired left-brained, some are wired right-brained, and a rare few are able to use both in perfect concert. The ability to simultaneously use right-brain creativity and left-brain logic is thought to be the reason Einstein was such a genius.

That link between the right and left brain is what we're most concerned about here. The part of the brain that connects the two hemispheres is called the corpus callosum. The corpus callosum is responsible for transmitting neural messages between both the right and left hemispheres, helping us to write songs.

Two Brains

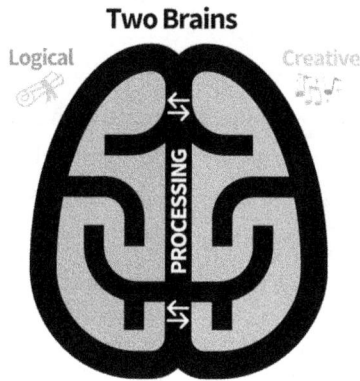

For example, as songwriters, we can match melody to the meaning of the lyric (prosody) to enhance the emotional impact of the song. At the same time, we can use our logic and creativity to be more productive in how we approach the songwriting process.

There's a brilliant discussion about this in one of my favorite songwriting books, the first one I found by the fantastic songwriting author Sheila Davis. In her book *Successful Lyric Writing*, she talks about "How to Put it Together" — that is, the left and right brains.[1]

In short, the fact that you are a songwriter means that you are likely to be a creative person in some way or another, and in that way, you are likely to have a strong right brain. But even with that assumption, there is a lot of variation in how songwriters can be wired. Ask yourself:

1. Are you a more creative idea/imagination-focused person? If so, you're likely right-brained. You may have piles of paper around the house in different places, but you might need some help to find your ideas.
2. Are you a more logical person who has little problem planning and setting goals? If so, as a left-brained individual, you might LOVE the idea of having written a great song,

but you might struggle with the experience of the actual writing process.

I know some creatives who are so creative that they hate the idea of anything left-brained. They say they aren't the right kind of Excel spreadsheet kind of people. They love living their lives by the seat of their pants and doing what they want to do whenever they want to. And if that's you, then that's fine! Enjoy, and good luck.

From my own experience, though, combining the best creative and logical approaches have been incredibly powerful. That was the case when I was in my corporate job as an equity analyst in investment banking as much as it is right now as a songwriter, composer, producer, and author. Many of the tools I used to use — Excel and Word, my iPhone, and laptop — I still use, and for the same general purposes.

Remember, the more creative you are as a songwriter, the more critical it is to figure out how to organize yourself as a songwriter.

And that's what this book is all about: enabling you to enjoy the writing process as much as possible at the same time as making the most of the ideas, songs, tools, and co-writes to allow you to move forward with your songwriting journey.

So, it's time to take a look in the mirror. Do you see someone exhibiting more right-brained or left-brained traits and habits? Understanding that will help you get to know just what problems you might face in becoming an organized songwriter.

WHAT DOES A PROFESSIONAL SONGWRITER DO?

I was recently emailed from one of my lovely readers, who asked,

---

"What — exactly — does a professional songwriter do? I mean, each day, what do you do?"

This is an excellent question! And to be honest, the work of a professional songwriter is very different from how other professionals spend their time. This is because, in reality, there is no definitive job description for songwriters, but they end up doing both what they love doing and what they can do best. Some love writing musicals, some love production, some love pop music, and some love choral. The lovely thing about songwriting is that you can do pretty much what you love doing.

The whole thing that makes a pro songwriter into a pro songwriter is that they approach it very much like many people who are in all professional jobs: they take it very seriously.

So, what does "seriously" really mean for songwriters?

I usually answer by talking about what I see as the three legs to this table. A professional songwriter who approaches their craft seriously spends their time working on each of these three areas:

- **Craft**: Taking time learning their craft, from reading books — like you are! — to investing in courses (e.g., Berklee College of Music). This also includes time spent honing their craft with regular practice (whether that's every day or every week).
- **Network**: Connecting with other individuals in the industry, including other songwriters, co-writers, artists, musicians, producers, publishers, management, PRO contacts (e.g., ASCAP), and individuals at industry events.
- **Technology**: Learning whatever technology they need to use, including everything needed for recording (DAWs), mixing, mastering, distribution, etc.

In the next few chapters, we will inevitably talk about how to approach all of these in more detail. But in my experience, a songwriter needs to equally emphasize these three categories.

When someone takes these above three categories all very seriously, it's evident for everyone around them that they are not just doing *an OK job at their work* as a songwriter — it's obvious that they are doing *their BEST job at their work.*

Pros understand what makes their craft work. They know what parts of their craft they don't know and what things they are best at. They know what and how to add value to their work. They know what songs are most likely to be taken seriously — not just by their Mom (even though that never hurts, certainly) but by publishers, artists, and other people they work with.

Before I started in my favorite career — songwriter, if you haven't guessed — I had several jobs that were very different from the job I finally landed on. I started working a day job as a chartered accountant (like a CPA), then worked in a financial role at Shell Petroleum and as an investment banker at UBS and Dresdner Kleinwort. Eventually, I ended up taking a six-month sabbatical to decide whether I wanted to be a full-time songwriter or not. And of course, right through to the very last day of those six months, I knew I couldn't go back to my corporate job, even though I'd had a successful career in various roles.[1]

But why am I bringing up my other jobs? Well, every time I changed my career (not just a change in jobs, but different work entirely), the same approach was required to make it work: craft, network, and technology. Even though each career change brought massive changes, I was able to make it through because I understood those three legs of the table. I think that was why the move to songwriting was relatively smooth: I was somehow trained to do that kind of move before, in my day job.

In short, whatever work you've done, whatever journey you have had to get to where you are in your songwriting journey, make the most of everything you have learned on your journey. Whatever kind of professional you've been in the past, you would do well to bring the skills you've learned to your work as a songwriter.

Look at my path as an example. You might think corporate work is as far from songwriting as you can get, but I find my experience with corporate work to be incredibly helpful as a songwriter. For one thing, I gained a great deal of experience working with left-brained tools and domains, including:

- Mind maps
- Spreadsheets
- Word processing

- Programming software
- Contracts
- Legal
- Accounting and finance
- Marketing
- Selling
- Purchasing
- Technical work

Of course, these benefits aren't limited to the corporate world — whatever your career path, many of the skills and abilities you have honed during your work outside of songwriting will almost certainly somehow be helpful in your work as a songwriter. If you have a lot of experience sending letters or other communications in your work outside songwriting, that will be a skill you will use every time you have to send a message as a songwriter. If you review contracts, you'll be glad to have that experience when you're getting signed with a publishing company. It's amazing what skills you'll find yourself using as a songwriter!

Sure, you certainly need to be creative in your work as a songwriter, probably more creative than your current day job. But sometimes it's just as uncreative getting the admin done as a songwriter as it was in any other job. You will always be able to dip into whatever work you've done before in your job as a songwriter.

SONGWRITER COMPETENCIES

As I said, many of the skills and abilities you have honed during your work outside of songwriting will almost certainly somehow be helpful in your work as a songwriter. But in our industry, there are many competencies (i.e., the ability to do something successfully or efficiently) that are a necessary part of being a songwriter. For example:

- Some professional lyricists might not be as strong as others in writing music, but they can be incredibly good at writing books.
- Some professional musicians might not be as strong as others in writing lyrics but are incredibly good at composing music for film and TV.

Here's the thing, though: just because we may feel we have strength in certain areas, it doesn't mean we can't go back to school and work to gain those competencies to enable us to improve ourselves, and that holds true for songwriting, too. (I'll be talking about this more in Part 3.)

For example, as soon as I quit my day job in investment banking, the first thing I had to do was to go back to school (Berklee Music School) to develop my skills in songwriting, music production, music business, arrangement, and music for film, TV, and games. I also found the best voice tutors I knew (Carry and David Grant) just to be able to compete with the incredible talent that exists in Nashville and elsewhere.

So if you're seriously considering stepping up your songwriting game, you'll want to do the same thing I did: identify areas needed to gain competencies, then go about getting yourself educated in that. Here's a picture of possible competencies you might want to consider if you had the opportunity to develop your skills - see more at Berklee Music School:

Competencies

Craft	Network	Tech
Lyrics	Co-writers	Demos
Music	Publishers	Acoustics
Creativity	Artists	Programming
Artistry	Industry	Engineering
Voice	Management	Production
Instruments	Financial	Label
Performance	Marketing	Recording
Arranging	Legal	Mixing
Composing	Film & TV	Mastering
Filling the well	DJing	Sampling
Orchestration	Education	Carpentry
	Leadership	Scores

Many master painters had many different skills to bring to bear on their work. For example, the Dutch painter Rembrandt van Rijn was also a draughtsman and printmaker. Leonardo da Vinci was famous for his painting, drawing, and sculpting, but also had interests and competencies in many other kinds of work, including invention, architecture, science, music, mathematics, engineering, literature, anatomy, geology, astronomy, botany, and cartography.

Not only did these artists have multiple areas in which they could find employment or realize their ideas, but they had broad expertise they could draw on in any of their pursuits. The more skills and competencies you've developed, including ones outside of songwriting, the more perspectives you can bring to your craft: the deeper and broader ideas, emotions, stories, conversations, and important pictures you can use when you write your songs.

EVERYTHING COMES THROUGH PRACTICE

There's a phrase in a song I wrote last year, which drives me now more than ever:

Never, never, ever give up on you.

ALL THE WORDS

A true story

When I left my day job, I knew I needed to have a goal. Not a normal thing for songwriters, maybe, but I knew how to write a business plan, so I thought I ought to do that for this new career. I gave myself five years from leaving my day job as a high-flying investment banker to achieve my dream. If a major music publisher hadn't signed me by then, I would go back to my old post again, if they'd have me.

After a lot of work (with the help of Berklee Music et al.) I was signed by a Nashville publisher, Brentwood Benson, part of Sony Music (now part of Universal Music). I had achieved my goal! I was thrilled to be working in my dream field, and I got plenty of congratulations from my former day job colleagues.

But there's more to this story.

A call

Just after I was signed, I got a call from someone from my former corporate day job. This colleague had a friend of a friend (actually a friend of his daughter at school) who was trying to accomplish the same thing, but he was a lot younger than I was. Since I'd had done a similar thing and made it work, he wondered if I'd listen to a CD of his songs and give my honest feedback. Of course, I agreed right away — on my journey, I'd been given a lot of help from people along the way (for which I'm still hugely grateful), so I was only too happy to do the same.

A few days later, sure enough, I received a CD and a letter from the father of this young songwriter, asking for whatever help I could give. As promised, I gave it a listen.

This was his first CD, one that he'd recorded at the house of a friend who was keen to help, just like I would have done. The songs were... well, OK. They were never going to make it in the charts, but there were a few pointers I gave to help him on his way. He was still in his mid-teens and so still under pressure to do well in his exams at school. Plus, he didn't have exactly the kind of look the charts would have been looking for: he was a young, chubby boy with messy ginger hair, wearing baggy jeans, a T-shirt, and a hoodie.

However, several things made him stand out from other musicians:

- He left school at the age of 16 to follow his songwriting work.
- He spent a lot of time gigging in London even though he didn't have money to afford it.
- He treated songwriting as his work, not a hobby.
- He realized he needed to be different from other artists.
- He spent as much time as he could to move his work forward.

So, after I had given him whatever my suggestions were on his songs, his father kindly emailed me to say thank you for that.

Now, can you guess the identity of this young up-and-comer?

Ed Sheeran.

Despite the success he ended up achieving, at the time, I knew that when I heard that first CD, it was not great writing. And I knew that there was a lot of work needed to move from writing OK songs to top-charting songs. But that's just what he did: he worked, and worked, and worked. Not just once a week but pretty much every hour, every day he could. Not just his craft, but he worked his network and his technology, as well.

And after more work than most people would even think about spending on songwriting, it paid off, big-time.

As of October last year, Ed Sheeran was the 17th-highest-earning British musician, with a net worth of £160 million. From 2006 to 2019, he went from just OK to that kind of success.

By now, it should be clear that if you put enough time and energy into your songwriting work, it can turn into something special. So if you love your craft, like all things: never, ever give up on it.

Nurturing the spark

In his autobiography *A Visual Journey*, Ed said:

"I'm proof that people aren't born with talent. If you listen to my early recordings, I can't play the guitar and can't really sing or write music very well either. It's all come through practice; everything comes through practice. You start off with a little spark, and it's whether or not you nurture that spark. You have to expand it and work on it."

ED SHEERAN

Is Ed's success due to me? Probably not. Even though I love to think it would have helped him along his way, but that's not why I write books anyway. I write books about how to write songs because anyone on their journey is on the same journey as I am. I've been helped so much by other people on this journey; if I can help in any way, then it's a privilege to be able to do that. We are all nurturing our spark, whether they are a glimmer or a flame.

So, how can we nurture that spark, to turn our ideas into finished, cut songs?

THE FORMULA

Many people have asked me how long it takes to get a first song cut. For me, it all comes down to a formula. Yes, it looks like left-brained math, but don't let that scare you; it's not really a formula since so many of the factors are so subjective. But the truth is, several things can affect which song gets cut.

Remember, this is just a formula based on my observations in the industry, not a guarantee. But it does hold true for most songs, I find. Here's the formula:

The Formula

$$J = nS \times (A\text{-}S) \times R$$

| Journey | Many Songs | Awesome *less* Sucky | Random |

Let me explain a little more how this works:

- **J** is the journey — how long it takes to get a cut. It can be in years or months, depending on the other side of the equation.
- **nS** is the number of songs written. Simple.
- **A** is how awesome each song is.
- **S** is how sucky each song is.
- **R** is randomness.

The factor you'll have the most control over as a songwriter is the value of A (awesomeness) minus S (sucky-ness). The more on your journey, the more awesome your songs should be getting. The higher (A-S), the better the chance of cuts, and the more songs you write, the more likely they are to be awesome rather than sucky. Then add in some randomness, hard work, networking, and technology, plus God's help, too.

My experience

For example, when I was beginning my songwriting career, my songs sucked. Yes, honestly, my songs were not good. My personal (A-S) was 100% sucky. As I put in a lot of work, though, writing many songs along the way through the Funnel (see Part 5), that (A-S) got better, gradually. And with a lot of help from my co-writers, a lot of courses, a lot of time with my family, and God's help along the way, I finally got my first cut. It took a long time, but this is how I nurtured my spark.

So is there anything a new writer can do to cut down the time needed to get a song cut? The short answer is yes! Just do these two things:

1. Do everything you can to cut down (A-S). In other words, write as many songs you can, and make them as awesome as possible.
2. Network, network, and network again (because otherwise, no one will know).

It sounds simple, but it is doable. As I said at the beginning of this book:

"Nothing is undoable. Just things not done."

So, by taking as many songs as possible from idea to recognition and making them more awesome than they are sucky, the more successful a songwriter will become. And that can totally be you if you're not already there.

Summary

In this part of the book, we've looked at the importance of having our own "why" for songwriting. We learned about how our passion for our work interacts with our natural mental tendencies and the experiences we've accumulated over our lifetime. We also covered the three legs of the songwriting table, the formula for getting songs cut, what it means to be professional as a songwriter, and how various songwriting competencies and other skills and abilities outside our work can be incredibly helpful to our craft.

In the next part, we are going to get a lot more practical: where do ideas come from, the importance of the Idea Bank — one of the most important tools for a songwriter, how to turn fresh, raw ideas into commercial, useable writable ideas and how to organize your writing, demo, and a whole load more. Keep reading!

Exercise

If you have a copy of *The Organized Songwriter's Workbook*, this would be an excellent time to complete Exercises #1-4.

PART TWO

HOW TO ORGANIZE IDEAS AND SONGS

"To have everything, everywhere."

THE SONG CHAIN

Ideas are where all songs start. Some genres are not really about lyrics, but they still need to have great musical ideas to make a successful song. Similarly, some genres are not about the music but still need a great lyrical idea to make it work. Without a great idea behind the lyric or a fantastic musical idea, songs are unlikely to go anywhere, much like the early work of Ed Sheeran, I mentioned in the previous part of this book.

Of course, if we happen to put together a great lyric idea **AND** a brilliant hooky melody, we've got the best chance of success. (Whatever that means to you.)

Think of songs like "I Will Always Love You" by Dolly Parton, made famous by Whitney Houston, or "Leaving On A Jet Plane" by John Denver. Then, there's one of my favorites, the most powerful lyric written by Phil Coulter and sung by Sinéad O'Connor called "Scorn Not His Simplicity." The thing I love about these is that, whatever the genre or subject, you can see it's just an incredibly well-crafted song starting with their first idea.

In this section, we are going to get a lot more practical. I'll cover where fresh ideas come from, the importance of the Idea Bank — one of the most important tools for a songwriter — how to turn raw ideas into viable commercial ones, and how to organize to get down to writing, demo, and a whole load more. Finally, I will introduce a second songwriter's secret weapon, which will help move your songwriting towards getting your work cut. Keep reading!

Why Organize?

I'm going to be honest with you now: some people just don't like to be organized. It might sound harsh, but it's true. Even part of me doesn't like being organized, sometimes. There are days I love giving myself a lovely creative day off. However, doing creative work is still doing work. Even if I'm focusing purely on the creative side of things, it's not actually a day off. It's a day working, and that means doing something that needs organizing.

But here's the good news:

"Organized work is a lot less effort than unorganized work."

Most times, organized work is incredibly productive. And, given the right focus on the right tasks, it takes less time to do organized work. Even the task *of organizing work* sounds like it's going to take a lot of time in the first place, but it really doesn't. Sometimes, deciding what to do with a fresh idea can be done in less than five minutes, especially if you are able to capture *that feeling* or emotional juice behind it.

The difference between being organized and disorganized (or chaos) is the key for us creatives. Being organized makes it possible to add significant creative value and do something positive with the idea.

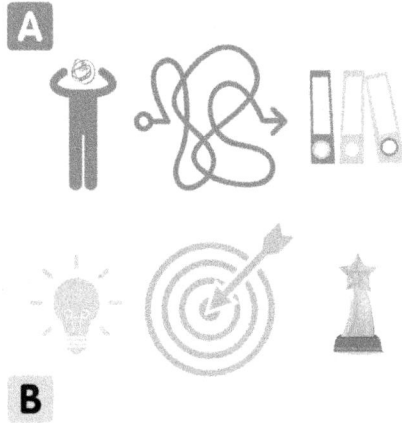

If you're organized, you'll have the energy to expend the effort to think, "What can I do with this fresh idea?" You'll be able to take fresh ideas through a process that will enable the fresh idea to grow into a writable idea, then plan to write it into a finished song at some stage in the future. Or it can be about taking an amazing writable idea and organizing a co-write.

In other words, whether we are left-brained or right-brained or somewhere in between, we can gain a lot by having the things and processes we need to organize ourselves as songwriters.

In reality, organizing ourselves as writers is a lot about having all the right data in the right place. Having used this approach, getting organized as a songwriter, is one of the main reasons I ended up getting signed at Brentwood Benson/Universal Music. It enabled me to turn piles of paper into songs that were ultimately cut as commercial songs as a staff writer and helped me become more productive and meet my publisher's equity quota of songs. And more importantly, it helped me turn many ideas into finished songs, ones that ended up being recognized, allowing me to receive awards and nominations from Doves to GRAMMYs.

So now that you know why you need to get organized let's help you figure out how. We can start by learning about the means by which songs go from idea to smash hit: the Song Chain.

The Song Chain

I'd like to introduce you to something new: the **Song Chain**. There are several different stages, or links, in the life of a song, from fresh ideas to recognition. Each link of the song has some kind of value-added component to it. There are many ways of looking at this, but I like thinking of it in terms of 12 links in the chain:

Creative

- Fresh idea
- Writable ideas
- Draft lyric
- Draft music
- Work tape
- Delivered

Commercial

- The demo
- Pitching
- The cut
- Releasing (by the artist/group)
- Marketing
- Recognition (GRAMMY!)

Here's what it looks like as a picture.

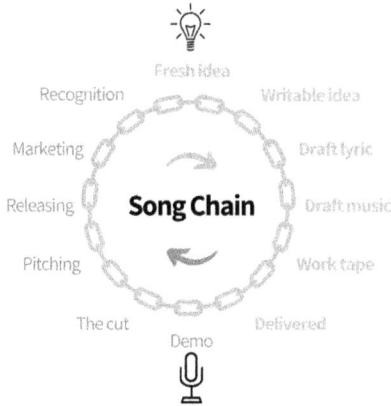

Creative

As songwriters, we have a lot more to do with the first half of the chain than the second half, from fresh ideas through to presenting a song to publishers. (That is unless we are a musician or working with an artist/group ourselves. Yes, people working close to artists/groups also write songs that get cut.)

For those only doing songwriting, it's more about us adding the creative value into the song. For the publisher, artists/groups, and labels, it's more about adding financial value to the song. But either way, value is being given to the song at each step.

Let's look at each link in a little more detail.

1. Fresh idea

At the very beginning, a song starts with a fresh, raw idea. The idea could be a lyrical idea (e.g., a title[1], a phrase, or even a theme or story) or a musical idea (e.g., a chorus or a hook), or even both together. But either way, this needs to make you think,

"Ooh, that could be a GREAT song."

Remember, the best ideas are those that have a meaningful hook. That's what makes you want to go back later and spend some quality time on it. And that's why it needs to be captured before it flies away like a butterfly.

An example of this was the idea I had for a song, "Fall." I was listening to the radio when I heard a short story that really resonated with me, something I could use in a possible song. So, I had to stop the car and capture it. Otherwise, it would have been lost, not taken to the next level: a writable idea.

2. Writable idea

Writable ideas come from taking the initial fresh ideas and developing them further, putting more meat on the bones of the idea developed in Step 1. It's when we figure out what the song could end up like — seeing the idea as a song. This is regarding the song in broad terms, an overview.

Going back to the example above, when I was at home, I took the idea for "Fall," but rather than writing the whole lyric, I simply attached a phrase or sentence to each section of the song.

In this way, it became ready to be written with a co-writer or on my own. It was not a written draft lyric, just a writable idea.

3. Draft lyric

In drafting the lyric, the aim is to take the writable idea to the next level and develop the lyric from this idea. Writing the lyric is one of my favorite stages in the song value chain.

"Fall" was one of those ideas that I nurtured for a few years until I knew it was ready. I was in Nashville and writing up with one of my favorite artists, and I knew I had a number of ideas like this to bring into the writing room. The lyric was easy to craft together, and the final version came out well.

4. Draft music

Composing music is also a beautiful stage for me. In reality, Steps 3 (lyrics) and 4 (music) can happen simultaneously or in reverse order. When I'm writing on my own, I often have to have a great draft lyric before turning to the music — the music is always there for me. However, for some people, it's the other way round. But, as I like to say, there's no rule, just tools.

When we co-wrote "Fall," we spent more time with the lyric before moving to the music. My co-writer was brilliant at both.

5. Work tape

By work tape, I don't mean an actual recording on tape. In this day and age, we don't (usually) use tape — it's just a term from the past. This step is about recording anything to get the idea of the song, with all the details as we can, to capture the song we've written. This is often done on a smartphone, a laptop, or whatever technology is handy and easy to use. The aim is to capture the drafted lyric and melody while remaining fresh in our minds before it is lost.

"Fall" was recorded on my Mac.

6. Delivered

Now that we have a song written, a lyric sheet typed out, and a work tape recorded, it's time to deliver our song to the world. This generally means presenting the song to someone — music is meant to be heard, not shut away in a drawer, after all. It could be submitted to a publisher, a chosen trusted creative person or, frankly, anyone we trust performing our songs. If the person to whom the work tape is delivered has some kind of meaningful feedback, be sure to listen.

The following day I delivered the work tape of "Fall," lyric sheet, and publishing details to my publisher, who loved the song. Thankfully!

FOR MANY SONGWRITERS, the first six stages of the Song Chain are the most fun and creative links of the Song Chain. In fact, some people love writing songs just for the fun of the above six steps. On my journey, even before getting signed as a published staff song-writer, I'd already written many, many songs — both on my own and with my first few co-writers. I'd also written many ideas into writable ideas, not yet finished into songs. Even before I'd been signed, it was still a brilliant stage of my journey, developing skills as a musician and a lyricist.

By the time I was signed by my publisher, I had a large back catalog of songs, which was signed to my publisher, too, as part of the contract. This is something worth thinking about if or when you get signed by a commercial publisher.

If you choose to do something more with your songs, here's the next few links in the Song Chain, from publishing to recognition. Much of this has been written with the perspective of a commercial songwriter creating songs with specific recording artists in mind, but the process is much the same across the industry.

Commercial

7. The Demo

THE DEMO SHOULD BE EXACTLY what it means: a demonstration. That is, it should sound just like the artist. Obviously,

- If you are the artist who is going to record the song, that's a lot easier!
- If you're writing for a specific A-class artist, the demo should be as close as possible to what they sound like. This means getting a great singer who sounds like them, musicians who sound like their band, and, especially, make sure the whole thing sounds like whatever genre they work in.

Holly, the Creative Manager at my publisher, had a great knack for finding the right session singers and musicians to enable the house producer, Barry Weeks, to deliver **AMAZING** demos. Note that great demos cost real money, normally charged to your account with your publisher. So, even if you have delivered many great songs to your publisher, it's only those that can be pitched by your publisher to a specific artist who is looking for songs that get demoed.

In reality, a great demo can sound a lot better than even the final artist. It's nearly always a wonderful moment to hear your demos finished. So enjoy it!

8. Pitching

Pitching songs is another art in itself. Pitching is connecting with artists, management, producers, record label people, and/or other publishers and playing your songs in the hope that they will record your songs. There's a great blog post on The Dos And Don'ts Of Pitching Your Songs In The Music Business by Marty Dodson on SongTown.com, which is very helpful if you want to pitch your own songs. One of the things he mentioned was:

"Make sure that your song fits what the artist is looking for VERY closely."

MARTY DODSON

I know I mentioned it above under Step 7, but it's important to make sure the song fits. Not just a bit like it, but VERY closely like it.

I love this blog because while there are some important don'ts, pitching is still something we can do as a songwriter without even being signed to a publisher.

9. The Cut

The cut is when an artist or group records a song. These last few stages of the Song Chain become more and more outside of the song-writer's control unless they are the artist. And even then, they might not have much control!

For songwriters, getting the cut is ultimately the most important thing to happen. After all:

- It helps pay the bills.
- It increases our credibility as songwriters.
- It makes us realize we are writing songs of importance, and
- It encourages us to continue working as songwriters.

Apart from writing a killer song and making sure the demo is also spectacular, the actual cut itself is mostly uncontrollable. There were some cuts I thought were in the bag that made it to the final project. Yay! On the other hand, I've written and had demoed what I consider some of my best work as a songwriter, and they haven't even been on a project at all. This happens. In fact, not having songs is more the norm than everything being cut. It's part of the life of a songwriter, and we need to be OK with that. In Part 5 of this book, I talk about the importance of celebrating the journey, even when the cut is bounced off a project.

10. Releasing

Releasing the project is down to the label, management, the producer, the artist/group, and even the media! But like with each step of the Song Chain, until the song on a project has been released, the highest value of the song has not been realized. But when it *is* released, there are a lot of people smiling — that, of course, is a time to celebrate as a writer.

Some people involved in the process find the actual release a difficult time for them. This is because, after being involved in giving birth to a creative product, after all the angst involved in getting it right on the day, after many months in nurturing a new baby, the release moment can be when the hype is over too quickly.

It's when the show is over, and it's time to work on another project, which might not necessarily be as great as this previous launch.

11. Marketing

Similarly, marketing has a massive impact on the value of the song. When it's done well, there is a much bigger revenue stream coming back to the ultimate owners (if not necessarily the creators) of the art. Unfortunately, for many years songwriters have not been adequately compensated for the incredible creative value they provide by writing songs. This has primarily been due to royalty fixed rates set for song-writers that are way out of date. This is changing, I believe, if slowly (I've still not yet seen this reflected in my royalty checks!).

With the huge impact technology continues to have on the industry in music and beyond, there are some important trends we can see happening. Still, this book is not about digital marketing for music. One of the best books about this is *How to Make It in the New Music Business by Ari Herstand*. Essentially, independent artists now have a massive opportunity to take control of this link in the Song Chain so they can own, promote, and market their music and build and manage their fan base.

12. Recognition

There are many ways to have your song recognized. While it's great to be nominated for a major award such as a Grammy or a Dove award, some of my most exciting moments have been from hearing my songs and hymns at my local church. Apart from the main industry awards, there are the main performance rights organizations (PROs) that present their own awards — ASCAP, BMI, SESAC, and SoundExchange in the US and the Ivors/PRS in the UK.[2]

The top of the chain

As songwriters, the further a song goes down the above twelve steps of the Song Chain, the less we can — in reality — control what happens to our songs. Giving our songs to a publisher is similar to saying goodbye to our children when they leave home. When you've done your best job with the song, it has its own life. That's why I see two different kinds of work for a song: creative and commercial.

Song Chain

1. Initial fresh idea
2. Writable ideas
3. Draft lyric
4. Draft music
5. Work tape
6. Delivered
7. The demo
8. Pitching
9. The cut
10. Releasing
11. Marketing
12. Recognition

↑ Creative ↓

↑ Commercial ↓

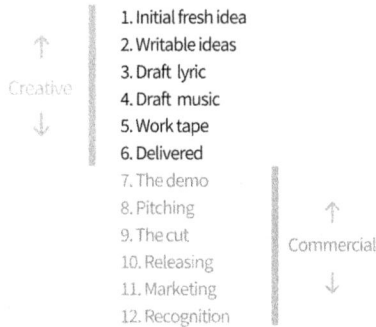

The first kind of work — creative work — is what I'm most interested in as a songwriter. This is the artistry invested in the product, the quality of the ideas found and used, the pictures being painted in the lyrics and music, the emotional payoff, and the skill of our craft that has been invested into our work.

Many songwriters spend most of their time in those top six creative steps. However, some songwriters choose to get involved in further steps of the chain, into commercial parts of the process. For example,

- Even though one of my co-writers is signed as a staff writer at a major music publisher, they are also very involved in demoing and pitching their songs to artists and management.
- I have several co-writers who are artists/writers who have been most involved in the last six steps, as well as the first six. If my life were to mean performing 250 gigs a year, I would want to have a say in the material, too!
- I have some co-writers who are producer/songwriters and have a strong view of what kind of material is needed. That's helpful.
- I have a couple of co-writers who are also label managers.

They are rare (for some reason), but they love being involved in the whole chain, from idea through to recognition.

The question for all of us as songwriters is this:

"What part of the Song Chain do you want to be involved in?"

Many would love to be totally focused on the creative work — Steps 1 through 6. However, many get involved in other parts of the chain simply to put bread on the table. Everyone has their own journey.

But the Song Chain isn't the only tool you'll need to understand to make it as a songwriter. You'll also want to start using an essential tool in my songwriting tool kit: the Idea Bank.

THE IDEA BANK

The Idea Bank is a wonderful thing for songwriters and other creatives. Some people might have a hook book or other systems of capturing their ideas, and that's fine. But the Idea Bank is much more than just a hook book.

An Idea Bank is where you can organize all your ideas, completed songs, and a whole load more to make sure you can be productive, prolific, and happy. It's a way to be sure that it's all there where you need it as a creative person when you need it. It's your stuff — all of it — in one place.

The Idea Bank was born after many courses about songwriting at Berklee Music School and after many trips to Nashville. It came after I realized I was losing too much key information as a songwriter. And I needed too many lists on pieces of paper, random emails, and various different spreadsheets.

Key information included:

- What are my most powerful writable ideas?

- Which co-writer might want to write each writable idea?
- When am I co-writing with whom?
- How close was I from meeting my publisher's quota?
- What are the publishing details for my co-writer?
- Where can I find all the information my publisher needed *after* my trips?
- And a million other things

I realized I needed something better than just a lot of lists on paper. Something that was better than a lot of spreadsheets (which was my normal solution in my corporate life!). I needed some kind of data-base, ideally, that I didn't have to enter a million different places. Yes, a relational database. And that's when the Idea Bank was first formed.

Why have an Idea Bank?

The Idea Bank has been an important tool for me over the years. It has allowed me to access all of my ideas wherever I am. It has also helped me turn up ready to serve my co-writers as best I'm able to. There is nothing better than arriving for a co-write with a full pool of great, well-thought-out ideas in mind for your co-writer. There's nothing better than seeing a co-writer's face light up and say, on hearing the first or second idea,

"I'd LOVE to write that!"

This is the aim of the Idea Bank: starting with all of your writable ideas. Your Idea Bank is where you can go, even before you walked into a writing session, to select from a wealth of possibilities. To have already answered the inevitable question you will (almost certainly) be asked:

"So, what ideas should we write today?"

That's when your Bank comes to your help with a number of really inspired ideas you and your cowriter will want to write.

After a time, you may have some writable ideas in mind for certain co-writers. Or you may well have a number of five-star ideas that you just can't wait to write. This is why having an Idea Bank is important.

What can be included in the Idea Bank?

There are many things you can include in your Idea Bank — everything from notes to your co-writer's publishing details. But having used this tool, using different versions and iterations over time, there are now five core sections of my own Idea Bank:

- **Captured** — fresh ideas
- **Writable** — ideas mapped
- **Organized** — what, when, why, and who
- **Written** — draft songs
- **Delivered** — finished, recorded, and cataloged

Idea Bank

Captured

↓

Writable

↓

Organized

↓

Written

↓

Delivered

Whatever form your Idea Bank takes, the general idea is to keep all your work as a songwriter — from the barest hints of ideas to drafts that are finished and turned in — in one place. As a fresh idea (captured) is worked on, it gradually changes status from captured to writable, organized, written, and, ultimately, delivered. More on each step of this process below. Ready to get your own Idea Bank started?

1. CAPTURED

Captured ideas are fresh, raw ideas. Ideas are the source of our song-writing.

When gold is being panned, they need to capture a large quantity of ore and water, which are carefully processed before, gradually, the gold is left at the bottom of the pan.

Dealing with fresh ideas is much the same. Those initial ideas are fresh material, from which you can find everything that might be used in the future. The trick is to capture everything, everywhere, then at a later date, you can find out which ideas are worth writing. This is how we find our golden song ideas.

Where do fresh ideas come from?

Have you ever been asked,

"What's your favorite song?"

Or,

"What's the very best song you've written?"

Nine times out of ten, unless you've already prepared for the question, it's very difficult to come up with an answer off the top of your head. I'm not sure why that is the case, but it just works like that.

It's the same thing with writing a song. If you were to go into a co-write and were asked,

"What's your best song idea, then?"

It would be just as difficult to come up with a great idea off the top of your head unless you've had a chance to properly prepare for it. If you're asked that question, you might feel like you're back at school, in your final exam. And so before a writing trip to Nashville, that's what I always do: prepare.

(Note: while I know some songwriters have been asked that question in a co-write, it's not something I've been asked myself, thankfully. Let's face it; it's a pretty aggressive approach in what is normally a nice comfortable environment to write in!)

But leaving aside identifying your best idea, let's look at the bigger questions: where do ideas come from? And how do you find them? My view is as follows:

They are everywhere.

Yes, the reality is that ideas are everywhere. And they arrive just when they want to arrive, not when it's convenient for us. Not even when you need it. Actually, I find they mostly arrive at the most inconvenient time. But whenever they arrive, that's when they need to be captured.

For example,

- I can jump into bed after a crazy busy day, and for some reason, a great song idea will just arrive. I never asked it to arrive; it just did. Or
- I could just have gotten into the shower when, yes, another idea can arrive, without me asking for it or being ready to write it down.

Honoring fresh ideas

This happens all the time. What matters, for us as songwriters, is what do we do with them when they arrive? Do we a) Tell the idea to come back later when it's more convenient? Or b) Simply capture it?

As I said in my last book on this topic:

"I'm not sure how to prove what I'm about to say. All I know is that from my experience, it's as true as the sun will rise tomorrow morning. It's this:

The more you honor your song ideas, the more ideas will arrive.

What I mean by "honor" is when an idea arrives, whatever you are doing, wherever you are, whoever you're with, capture it and put it somewhere safe.

There have been seasons in my life when my focus has been less on writing and more on other work, traveling, living in a dangerous place (Nigeria, but that's another story). During these seasons, I have found that ideas gradually start to turn up less and less often.

It's almost like I've taken off my 'songwriter ears' for a time, and until I make a real effort to put them back on again, I'm deaf to the golden song possibilities my subconscious will lead me to in the everyday, ordinary things of life.

SONG MAPS, CHAPTER 3

And the more ideas we capture, the more ideas flow.

How do we capture ideas?

There really are no rules about how to best capture a fresh idea — you can literally use **any** tool to capture an idea in any shape or size. From my experience, I've used everything from beer mats to cafe napkins to pads of paper to anything else.

I started writing when I was about eight years old. And when I started songwriting, even though I didn't really call it that, I never had any kind of system or set of notes, a hook book, an audio recorder, or anything like that at all.

I was just having a bit of fun, playing the piano and singing some words I thought might work, albeit in a quiet, nervous way. And why not?

Then, when I actually starting to writing more purposefully, I realized I was losing so many ideas — I just couldn't remember all of the great ideas I was trying to remember for writing because I had no way to capture them. And that was a problem I needed to do something about.

My first notes

My first "notes" were not very good in terms of quality, quantity, or organization. They were mostly pieces of paper I found somewhere close to me: a flyer from my brother's business, a napkin from a restaurant, even a beer mat. Mostly they were pieces of paper that were just lying around. As I got more into songwriting, though, and began taking it a lot more seriously, my best investment for a long time was:

- A pad of paper
- A ring binder
- A three-hole punch
- A clipboard

Although this system was simple, it worked great and kept me going for a long time for several reasons:

- It was somewhere I could keep all of my work safe.
- I started a system to help me find things in some sort of order.
- Whether I'd written an idea on this pad of paper or on a sheet of toilet paper, I was able to have access to all of it in my file.
- In fact, this system worked so well that I still have all my notes from this period, filed and ready to use!

This worked great for capturing lyrical ideas and even for capturing some of my melody ideas to a limited extent. To be honest, I wasn't that great at writing music on paper, so I needed an additional investment: a cassette recorder. That was perfect, but I still needed to somehow log these in some way if they linked to the lyrics I'd written (which wasn't always the case).

So I started two lists: One list for lyrical ideas and one list for music ideas. And they were linked to one another so I could make sure I knew which I wanted to live together. And that worked, sort of.

More sophisticated notes

Using this system, I found capturing musical ideas was fine – I was always able to find music whenever I needed it, and I was able to capture that. But the lyrical ideas were still not what I needed. This is because I wasn't actually listing proper lyrical ideas, just a list of simple subjects, rather than lyrics themselves – ideas for what songs would be about that I thought might be "appropriate" to write about. And as time went on, though, I realized I needed to capture something much more than that. I needed to capture something more tangible, proper lyrical ideas, such as:

- Cool turns of phrase
- Whole lines that could become part of the lyric

- Key moments for emotions or meaningful ideas
- Titles I'd not heard before
- Titles I'd heard, but I knew I could write in a different way[1]
- Musical choruses or other sections
- Hooky intros or motifs
- A cool drum and bass idea, even without a melody

So my journey went from having ideas disappear as soon as they came to me to capturing all of my song ideas, both lyrical ideas and musical. Once I did that, I found they were there, everywhere. As long as I had my file.

As time went on and technology advanced, I migrated my paper file onto an Excel spreadsheet and onto Word docs, and that was great too. I'll talk a lot more about technology in the next part of this book, Tools of the Trade, but suffice to say the technology today is amazing. I love being paper-free and love, finally, having achieved what I mentioned above: to have access to everything everywhere. And that's where I am today.

My ideas box

OK, there's something I need to confess: I know I said I'm paper-free, but I still have one thing that I sometimes use:

My Ideas Box.

And this is what it looks like:

Yes, it's where I capture all of my paper ideas. Despite all the advantages of technology, sometimes I still use paper if:

- I don't have my iPhone with me (rare)
- I see something in a magazine or a newspaper
- Someone writes me a paper note or letter
- I find a piece of paper (for example, in my attic or when I'm at my Mom's home)

I don't use my physical ideas box very often, and every few months or so, it all gets put into a different system and emptied, but it's great to have somewhere to store paper stuff before I can put it in the Idea Bank.

Capturing in my Idea Bank

So what do I do when I come upon a fresh idea? As you've probably guessed, I capture it in my Idea Bank.

For many years I've needed a database (FileMaker Pro), but as mentioned, I'll be talking about the technology I've found most helpful in detail in the next part of this book. But the important thing is what, exactly, is captured? In terms of data, this is what I capture:

- A working title
- Any lyrical elements of the idea
- Any musical elements of the idea
- Date created

Using paper or whatever technology I've worked with, I try to collect any and all of this data, then save it in my Idea Bank under the Captured section.

So now that we know what a fresh idea looks like and what to do with it, let's learn about the next step in the process.

2. WRITABLE

"Writable" refers to mapped ideas — that is, after sifting through your pan, these are the ideas that are gold.

Mapping writable ideas is one of the most fun parts of songwriting for me. Just for a moment, imagine we are searching for gold — real, physical gold. Gold, that's incredibly valuable when we find it. Imagine how we might pan for gold, moving a big dirty pan after filling it up with a lot of water and a lot of dusty ore, shifting it back and forward, gradually removing away the unwanted, unhelpful things. Until finally, we see what we're looking for: gold! There's still a lot of more work needed to make it a valuable nugget, but we have just what we need to get started.

This is exactly what we are doing in mapping writable ideas: we take a good look at all of our fresh ideas and move them around until we see something shining, something that could be just what we're looking for, something that we can turn into a commercial song. Among all the unwanted, unhelpful ideas, we need to look until we see what we are looking for: a writable idea! There's still a lot of work needed to write this song into a valuable nugget for people to sing. But once we find it, we can log it and get ready to write.

Writing in 3D, not 2D

Here's another way of looking at it. Many young songwriters usually write lyrics in just 2D. What do I mean by 2D? Well, it's not that 2D songs don't sound nice or are cool. But you can see a 2D lyric like the sun shining on a clear sky — a 2D lyric is flat. It doesn't move us from place A to place B. By the end of the song, we are still in the same place as when we started listening to it. Most lyrics in a 2D song simply say exactly the same thing again and again, using different words to describe the same thing. In other words, there are two dimensions:

- Title (or theme), and
- Structure

A 2D song might look like this in a graph:

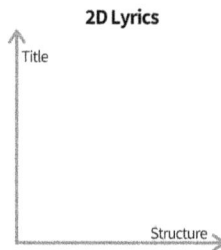

2D Lyrics

Title

Structure

Now, don't get me wrong, the fact that a song has a title or theme and a structure might lead many people to say, "Well done!" But when you look at the lyrics more deeply, you'll notice that whatever idea is in verse 1, the same idea is in verse 2, only with different words. And the bridge does exactly the same thing.

So what's missing? What element could make this 2D song come alive? How can we get to the end of the song and feel like we have really gone to a new different place — we are no longer in the same place we were in verse 1?

The power of plot

Writing a song in 3D is the work of pro lyric writers — that is, those who are committed to taking us to a different place with their songs. You may think I'm overstating the importance of this, but I always say it's like the difference between watching a black-and-white TV versus a color TV. It's like having a chat with your Mom on a landline telephone (if you can find one!) versus Zooming her on an iPad Pro.

So, what is the big difference? A song written in 3D provides a much clearer and complete picture. All three dimensions of a song are there:

- Title (or theme)
- Structure, **and**
- **Plot development**

In contrast to a 2D song, it would look like this in a graph:

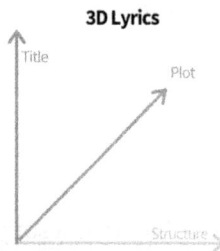

3D Lyrics

In songs written in 3D, lyrics show that the ideas in each section are different throughout the song. With every verse and chorus, they move the listener on a journey, recoloring each chorus or refrain, showing that with each step through the song, the story has moved on. Sometimes dramatically, with a cool payoff.

This is why I focus on Song Mapping in this step of organizing our songwriting. By the end of mapping a fresh idea, you can already see if this is going to be an OK song, or, if mapped well, it could be a brilliant song lyrically.

Where do we find writable ideas?

There are many different ways of sorting the writable ideas from our fresh ideas. In essence, we simply sift through our fresh ideas — whether they are single-word titles or cool phrases, musical hooks, or motifs — and make them come to life by figuring out what plot (*not* story[1]) can be made from that initial idea. It's about developing our fresh ideas. It's about seeing where the song could potentially go and making a judgment on the quality of gold we are looking at.

So again, there are no rules about how to turn fresh ideas into writable ideas. Everyone has their own personal magic.

However, what I **do** know is that Song Mapping is very much at the heart of my own way of turning fresh ideas into writable ideas. After four years with my readers, I feel safe saying this is a well-tested way to turn fresh ideas into writable ideas, many of which are well worth writing into finished songs.

This is what Song Maps are about, as introduced in my last book, *Song Maps — A New System to Write Your Best Lyrics*. Here's a passage from that book, when I talked about writable ideas:

"A writable idea, as I define it, is the combination of two things: a title PLUS a development strategy (= a Song Map):"

Writable Idea

$$\text{Writable Idea} = \text{Title} + \text{Development}$$

"So a title on its own is not a writable idea; it's just a title. If I were to go into a co-write with just a bunch of titles, there would be a massive random element as to whether we'd even come out of the session with a song. I believe that, to serve my co-writer well, I need to bring more than just a few titles into the room to justify them spending three hours with me, rather than with another writer who may well be better prepared.

Similarly, a Song Map on its own is not a writable idea. It needs to be put together with a title. A title that resonates with both my co-writer and me. The Map on its own is just a way of signposting how ideas flow around that title to recolor it, to expand it, to generate a payoff that somehow justifies the listener spending three to four minutes of their lives giving it some air time. And 99 cents of their hard-earned cash."

My last book goes into a lot of detail about what Song Maps are all about and how to use them. I'd totally recommend that book as well as the accompanying workbook. In both of those, however, I mention that writable ideas are key to making sure you have great ideas when you write, either on your own and especially in preparing for co-writes.

And how do you keep your writable ideas safe? You build your own Idea Bank!

Writable ideas in my Idea Bank

So, in my Idea Bank, I've got all the fresh ideas that I can map into writable ideas. What exactly does that look like? In addition to what already is there (like a working title, etc.), here's what I generally include in my Idea Bank:

- A Song Map or some other way of developing the fresh idea from a 2D to 3D lyric
- Updated lyrics and possible updated music

The cool thing about the Idea Bank is that now there is a very real chance of these writable ideas becoming real finished songs, including a 3D depth of the lyrics plus whatever musical notes I have. All I need to do now is decide a few things, and that brings us to the next step.

3. ORGANIZED

Organized ideas are writable ideas that have been *actually planned* for writing into finished songs.

While a lot of sifting has already taken place, this is still part of the sifting process. That is, we're still trying to find the gold among all the debris.

Four Questions

At this point, it's time to bite the bullet on writable ideas and ask a few quality-related questions. Specifically, we need to focus on:

- **Deciding**: Examine each writable idea to decide whether it's worth spending quality time on, to make it a real song. How strong is the writable idea? Is this something different enough to be worth spending time on? Has it been written before? What commercial (or other reasons) are worth spending time on it?

- **Firming up**: Having decided to move forward, it's time to firm up things about this idea. For example: what kind of genre would work best? What style could work well? What kind of timing (BPM, time signature)? Ultimately, you need to view how cool the idea is (give it a score out of 10) to help prioritize the ideas against each other.
- **Matching**: If we are writing this with a co-writer, who is best to write one particular writable idea? What do they love writing? Who likes certain genres or styles? Is there another co-writer who loves writing this idea? Ultimately, is this something I could credibly pitch to my co-writer? When introducing a cool idea, you'll have to pitch it enough to make it sound as good as it can be and show your co-writer they have an opportunity to add their magic to it.
- **Timing**: These are the logistics. When is this song going to be written or co-written? Note that there's unlikely to be a 100% chance of your own ideas written in every co-write.

Overall, these four questions are all about highlighting the best ideas we have in our Idea Bank. It's doing the homework so that when we arrive at a writing session, we have the best golden ideas that are worth spending time on. This is when we are able to change the status of a writable idea to an organized idea, ready to be written.

Now, sooner or later, you are likely to have a lot of writable ideas (I have about 500 in my Idea Bank). In reality, out of all of these writable ideas, there are some that always shout out to me before I'm writing. So don't feel you need to spend all of your time planning EVERYTHING!

As far as these four decisions go, here are a few tips:

- Sometimes, I don't have all the answers to these questions. That's fine, because it's supposed to be a tool to use as a creative person; it's not an exam. So feel free to keep some items blank.

- The cool score is a nice tool. It's there to help you give your subjective view on whether this idea has a high or low chance of ending up as a cut. The aim of this is to quickly scan through my ideas to see if there's anything that jumps out. You'll have to be quite strict about what scores you give. Otherwise, everything will be classed as a ten if you're not careful!

- Doing the process of matching ideas to possible co-writers is extremely helpful because a) it's likely to be necessary for a positive co-write, b) it's important to have the best ideas at the top of the list going into the co-write, and c) what's best for one co-writer is not necessarily best for another co-writer, so it's good to get your homework done early.

Sometimes I have one idea matched against several different future co-writers, and that's fine. Let me say a little more about that.

Never hold back

While I was talking to one of the professors at Berklee School of Music, I mentioned a quote that I always keep in mind during my co-writes:

> "Whoever you are co-writing with, never hold back your best song ideas."
>
> **PAT PATTISON**

Having all of my writable ideas available is incredibly helpful. It makes sure I have access to all of my potential writable ideas — from just OK to brilliant — so whoever I am about to co-write with, I am able to come up with something we can write about, even though we often end up writing their ideas or something completely new. I will talk more about this later.

As mentioned, right now, I have over 500 song ideas in my Bank, most of which are totally writable. The funny thing is, although I leave home for a writing session in Nashville with this number of ideas, I generally come back home with more writable ideas after my trip than when I went over. This is partly because:

- The 16-hour trip is incredibly helpful to consider more ideas on the way.
- Co-writing is not just about writing my ideas; it's about wanting to serve my co-writer as best I can, which often means writing their own ideas.
- Sometimes, in the chat, before we write, my co-writer and I will discuss many possible ideas before resulting in the idea we end up writing. I don't steal the ideas of my co-writers, of course, but during our journey, I'm always looking for possible ideas to write later.

See what kind of benefits come from having things organized? Not only do I have access to all my ideas wherever I go, but being so prepared equips me to pick up lots of new ideas as well.

Organized ideas in my Idea Bank

So, in my Idea Bank, what do organized ideas look like? Over and above all above, this is what I mostly focus on when moving ideas from "writable" to "organized."

- Song Map or development (if updated)
- Genre (options)
- Timing (signature)
- Style (BPM)
- Cool score (out of 10)
- Possible writing date (e.g., on a planned writing trip)
- Matching to possible co-writer(s)

Having made some critical decisions on these points, I shoot for bringing 5-6 credible, writable ideas to offer to my co-writers. There are always opportunities to review or change things around, but this is a great place to be in on my way to a co-write. The real fun part is now, of course, just writing it!

4. WRITTEN

Written songs are organized ideas that are in the process of being written. That is, written songs are works in progress (WIP), not quite finished. Yet, at least.

In reality, although I generally try to finish a song if at all possible during a co-write, it's not the end of the world if a song is left WIP at the end of a writing session. Different writers all have their way of doing this. I know one co-writer who takes three sessions before finishing. On the other end of the spectrum, I've written three complete songs in one session. There are no rules about this, of course. Personally, when I write on my own, I love keeping it open for more than a few sessions.

It's essential when organizing your work to keep track of songs that are WIP — otherwise, it's so easy to forget these little gems. And what's the point in writing something that gets lost? Remember, just because something is not finished doesn't mean it's not valuable — it could be the best song ever written. It just needs a little more love and energy to finish.

When is a song written?

Again, there are no rules about this, but for an idea to become written from organized, there needs to be some substantial work done on the idea. And that might mean just the last section is missing.

Many commercial writers like crafting a song in the following order. Note that this is a good order in which to approach writing a song, not the order in which these sections appear in the finished song recorded:

- Chorus (ideally identical each time)
- Pre-Chorus 1 (if appropriate)
- Verse 1 (maybe a double verse)
- Pre-Chorus 2 (if different)
- Verse 2
- Bridge
- Outro

Why write out of order like this? Well, I've found that sometimes after writing a great lyrical chorus, the music can be much easier to put together. I often end up writing both simultaneously or completing it easily after finishing that first chorus. The same thing often happens with other sections of the song until the whole song is totally drafted.

When working on a written song, I like to refer to this list and see if the song would benefit from having another section added or if the story of the song can be carried through the sections that are already written a little more clearly.

Of course, there are a million reasons why, even after going through this process, one of the co-writers might want to give this song a little space before coming back to it. And that's fine — some ideas take time. Just make sure you stay organized, or you could lose the gold you found!

All finished

One of the things I think is really important in co-writing is that everyone needs to be happy with the song. It's not like, if there are two out of three co-writers happy, it then gets turned in to their publishers. If someone is still not 100%, then there must be something somewhere that isn't quite right. And the whole point of co-writing is to have more eyes on a song to catch such problems, so it's always essential to make sure everyone is finished. Otherwise, I would keep it filed under Written, not Delivered in my Idea Bank.

At the end of the co-write, it's important to capture my co-writers' publishing details because there are few opportunities to talk about it. The written version completed becomes the final version that I send to my publisher.

Written in my Idea Bank

So, in my Idea Bank, what does a Written song look like? While the lyrics and music have changed since the previous step (because they have been written!), there are a few things important to capture after having written the song so far:

- Title (the final title)
- Lyric sheet (close to the final lyrics)
- Music (work tape)

- Actual writing date (e.g., on an actual writing trip)
- All writers' names, publishing details, and PRO
- Share (equity in the song finished[1])

It's a brilliant feeling to have written a great idea with the perfect co-writer for an idea I've captured earlier. Especially if there are specific possible opportunities for the song finding a home (cuts). But until it's actually given to a publisher or artist, it's still not going anywhere until it's delivered. And that's the next step.

5. DELIVERED

Delivered songs are songs that have been written, completed, recorded (work tape), and delivered as finished songs.

I always love this moment. Not because I don't like writing songs — I do — but because it means my catalog has grown by one more beautiful piece of work. It often takes a few days to listen to these songs again and figure out just how cool the finished product is. I often find they sound better than they initially sounded, with different impressions or cool twists I'd not yet heard.

Final version

It's **essential** to have a final version of your catalog available for the future. While a publisher should also have a copy of this final version, there are sometimes opportunities to pitch songs yourself, or you may find yourself being asked by your publisher about a particular song. It would be a nightmare to not have the fruit of all your work!

While I was a staff writer at Brentwood Benson/Universal, I liked turning in as many work tapes as possible to my publisher by the end of each writing trip. In reality, there were some trips that I just wasn't able to do, mostly because they were incredibly busy times. I also found it more important to prepare for my co-writes than do the admin work, which can be done when I get home.

On some trips, there were two or three co-writes per day over a couple of weeks - it's a lot of work but great fun!

Since having my own publishing outfit (Great British Music Publishing), I tend to give myself a little more time with this. I always do a work tape on my phone or in the studio when co-writing. But when I'm writing on my own, I like to spend more time on it — having everything on my iPhone, looking/listening to it often, and adding to it when fresh ideas come to me.

When is a song finished?

You would think that completed songs are all pretty straightforward. Well, yes and no. Here's what I mean:

- The finished song, in some ways, is never finished until it is cut. It's entirely possible that your publisher could come back to you with possible changes before they include your song in a pitch meeting. From my perspective, whenever I am asked, I **ALWAYS** try to do anything I can to help my publisher pitch my songs, if at all possible.
- Additionally, when turned in to a publisher (or even if you are your own publisher), a finished song has new information that needs to be logged at that stage. My publisher had a form (a Song Information Form or SIF) that

I still use every time I finish a song, whether I'm writing on my own or with any co-writers.

What goes on a SIF?

Here's what I include on the SIF:

- Final song title
- Date written
- Writers' names, publishers' details, PRO, and share percentage
- Possible pitches
- Possible samples used
- Music (work tape) with lyrics attached
- Email details

SIFs are linked to the song in my Idea Bank. This is for two major reasons:

- To keep track of where that idea went. Alongside this and other information about the completed song, I include a link to the finished lyrics and the work tape.
- To monitor where I am with my publishers' quota. Every songwriter signed with a publisher has a quota (equity share of songs written over a particular year), and this is an excellent way of keeping touch on this.

Delivered in my Idea Bank

So, in my Idea Bank, what does a Delivered song look like? In addition to the finished version of the song itself, I include details about where the song is likely to go:

- Updated final title
- Updated cool score
- Final co-writer(s) (sometimes additional final co-writers can be added)
- Final shares
- Possible demo
- Possible cut
- Possible project (artist/group)

I have well around 300 completed songs in my catalog, some from my time when I was at Universal/Brentwood Benson in Nashville and now from my own publishing. For each of them, I have a SIF filed in my Delivered section of my Idea Bank.

There is something nice about taking a look at your catalog and finding out how many songs you have written (equity share %) over the last year. The cool thing about having your Idea Bank updated with this data is that with a little technology, you can automate things. For example, generating and sending the SIF and how close I am to meeting my publisher's quota. Without this, it can be a real pain to do.

OTHER INFORMATION FOR THE IDEA BANK

In the previous sections, I've given some sample information you might want to include about each song that lives in your Idea Bank. In reality, though, there's no limit to what kind of information you can keep on your songs. It's all about getting whatever is needed to keep the admin as least painful as possible. In addition to what is detailed above, I also like to keep three additional kinds of information in my Idea Bank:

- Demos and cuts
- Co-writers
- Writing trips

Demos and cuts

To be honest, I don't demo all of my songs. In fact, I would say I probably only demo 50-60% of the songs I write. That's not because 40-50% of my songs suck (I think!) but because, from a commercial viewpoint, the songs that get demoed are those with the greatest chance of being cut. These songs could be demoed by a third-party producer, a home publisher's producer, or by myself, either recording everything myself or working with a Nashville voice or other recorded instruments.

Because I've always done a lot of work in my studio (more on this later), demos and cuts inevitably end up everywhere on my computer and iPhone. But this is also why I include these in one place — my Idea Bank. Not everything gets logged there; just the final version to have the best version available.

In the case of cuts, I capture a little more information alongside completed songs:

- Date of the cut (i.e., project release)
- The artist/group that cut it
- The project/album the song is included in

Co-writers

While capturing ideas, songs and cuts are very much part of our craft — managing co-writers is very much part of Network work. Honestly, "networking" feels much colder than these relationships really are; in reality, most of my co-writers have become very good friends. That's partly because they are genuinely great people to spend time with and partly because our songwriting is always a common interest. And at the end of the day, when we write lyrics and deal with real emotional issues, it's impossible to avoid knowing what a co-writer is all about. So, inevitably, co-writers become important, good friends. And it's always a privilege to spend time with these people.

In my Idea Bank, I have all the details of my co-writers as well, including basic data:

- Contact details
- Publishing details (PRO)

- Websites and blogs
- Photos (yes!)
- Number of songs written together and details of those songs, including cuts
- Possible ideas that they might like to co-write later

I currently have close to 100 co-writers with who I love spending time. They are more than co-workers; they are friends. Most of them are based in the US, mostly in Nashville, St. Louis, and California. They are relationships I value like gold, and I wish I could spend more time with them, especially right now.

Writing trips

Because I live in the UK and most of the musicians I co-write with are in the US, writing trips have always been a big part of my career. When I say "trip," I typically mean a physical journey to work with my co-writers. However, a writing trip could also be a video co-write given the incredible impact of technology and the not-so-wonderful impact of the current pandemic that limits travel.

Since I was first signed as a staff songwriter to Universal Music Publishing in Nashville, I regularly traveled the 20-hour, 4,181-mile trip from my home on the south coast of England to Cool Springs, Nashville, to co-write with other staff writers and artists.

I'd generally go five or six times a year, for a couple of weeks each time. While I was there (thanks to Holly Ward, my fabulous creative director), my calendar was often jammed with writing appointments — sometimes two or three a day. As I mentioned in my last book, Nashville is an extraordinary place. Not just because it's a mecca of incredible musical and lyrical talent, but also because it seems to operate on a different concept of time from the rest of the world: not Central Time, but what I jokingly call "Nashville-stretchy-time."

Let's just say that maybe 80% of the appointments on my calendar would actually happen.

Therefore, it was crucial for me to arrive in the writing room, ready to serve my co-writers well. The most stupid thing in the world would be for me to go to all that trouble and hassle only to arrive in the writing room with no ideas. Or even worse, with half-baked, clichéd, or sucky ideas. Therefore, I needed a consistent source of excellent, writable ideas and a robust system to find them behind it.

My Idea Bank is always incredibly important for my writing trips. Key data I capture for my trips include:

- Trip name (physical or video)
- When it starts and ends
- Which quota year they fell on
- What songs were written on each trip and important details about each song, including %, genre, tempo, and timing
- Co-writers
- Song status (co-writing, completed, SIF to a publisher)

I occasionally have some co-writes in the UK, and that's always a pleasure. If I co-write via video, it's normally after having written together face to face. That's why I love going to co-writing retreats. On some trips, there were two or three co-writes per day over a couple of weeks. My record is 21 new songs over a two-week trip. I've never been able to get more than that — it's a lot of work, but great fun!

Automated housekeeping

The reason I love having all of this data in my Idea Bank is that, given the wonders of technology, it's possible to automate so much of the housekeeping to allow me to focus on the creative value of song-writing rather than trying to keep track of everything on different spreadsheets or documents. It is truly wonderful to be able to input all of this data just once — each idea, song, co-writer, demo/cut, and trip —without needing to record it in a million different places. Plenty of other tasks can be automated as well, such as filling out and sending out SIF emails together with tracks and lyric sheets. But I'll be talking much more about this and how it's done in the next part of this book.

Ultimately, the aim of all of this organization work is to keep the housekeeping done as painlessly as possible. I hope you'll find that to be the case for yourself.

EXAMPLE: FALL

"Fall" is a great example of how organized ideas and songs worked well with the Idea Bank for me.

One Saturday morning, I was driving from my home in London to the south coast of England, listening to BBC Radio 2. Another DJ was standing in for my weekly favorite DJ. In fact, I didn't really like this character – he always came off as too full of his own opinions!

Halfway through the show, though, he started talking about his grandfather and how different his life had become after watching his grandfather falling down a few steps in his house. His grandfather was fine; it didn't hurt him at all. But it did make an impact on the DJ's view on life — things can change dramatically, just when you aren't expecting it.

Now, for some reason, it struck me that this would be a great idea for a song — a place or a timezone song — so I had to capture that idea, there and then. I felt a bit put out having to pull over the car and capture this story, but it just felt like I might need something about it.

It only took two minutes, and then it was done, and I got on with my journey.

Fast-forward to a few years later, when I found myself in my first co-write with one of my favorite artists, Cindy Morgan. Just before I embarked on my trip to Nashville from the UK, this song idea popped out of my Idea Bank as a possible co-write. As I got into the publisher's writing room, I briefly introduced this idea to Cindy, and the song "Fall" was borne. And it came out really well if I do say so myself.

The point of this story is how valuable it is to have a pool of ideas ready and available, just at the right time. I didn't know what would become of that idea when it first came to me, but because I had my Idea Bank system working well for me, it was hardly any trouble to save it for later. And sure enough, before too long, I had turned that stray idea into one of my favorite works.

Here are the lyrics to that song, so you can see how a captured idea can be transformed into a finished product:

Fall

Verse 1

It was fall, and I was ten

Racing sticks on the rivers' wind

The sun turned gold

And our hands turned cold

Across the train tracks

Past the corner store

It wasn't far

Then to his frosted door

Stood there knocking

I could hear him call

Then I saw something

At the end of his hall

I saw Grandpa fall

Chorus

He saw me there

Looking past the stairs

And when he got up from the ground

He brushed himself down

Verse 2

He was eighty with a young man's eyes

Wore his blue jeans and he rode his bike

Told me stories as we stoked the fire

He wasn't grand

But he was brave

He fought those dragons

That I couldn't slay

But like a knight

Falling off the wall

My childhood ended

At the end of his hall

When I saw Grandpa fall

Bridge

And as he smiled, so dignified

He opened up the door, we laughed, and we cried

Verse 3

Still, remember

After all these years

Down on the waxed floor

Where you meet your fears

When I go down

Like he did back then

Hope I know how

To get up again

Like he did

At the end of the hall

When I saw Grandpa fall

THE SONGWRITER'S SECRET WEAPONS II

To help you think more about how to make the most of capturing all ideas that will, almost certainly, arrive just when you are not expecting it, I thought it might be useful to share another secret weapon for songwriters.

In my last book, *Song Maps — A New System to Write Your Best Lyrics*, I mentioned the songwriter's #1 secret weapon: writing about love in the face of adversity. Having thought about the tools in my own songwriting arsenal, it occurred to me I have another good one to share, what I call the Songwriter's Secret Weapon II. (Of course, you could argue the Idea Bank is a pretty potent weapon for all songwriters, but that's not what I have in mind.)

At the start of my journey as a songwriter, I used to go to songwriters' conventions that would often have critiques of songs, where maybe 8 or 10 songwriting students and I would have our work judged and critiqued in public in front of everyone. Now, when I first heard about these, I thought they were nothing but horrific ideas — why would I ever want to allow my beautiful, newborn creations to be set up to be trashed and broken into pieces by these evil judges, setting out mass destruction in front of my peers? While that was not quite the case, some judges were indeed kind but harsh. But importantly, some were also excellent at giving the right kind of feedback that people could actually understand and get the point without leaving in tears — a kind of critique served up from within a sandwich of positive points.

I attended this convention not just to listen to my critique; I was hungry for all of these "critique sandwiches" for my own songwriting. And I heard one bit of feedback that was particularly helpful, the kind of secret weapon that I was able to use for much of my songwriting life. It was this:

Artists are not looking for songs in the middle of the table but songs that are:

At the edge of the table.

What does that mean? As I finally came to understand, the judge meant that if you take a circular table and point to the middle of the table, most songwriters are writing songs like that.

But judges, producers, and even listeners aren't interested in songs in the middle, but the songs at the edge of that table. Songs like that are different from all the rest, but not so different that they fall off the edge of the table entirely.

OK, so let's assume that's true. People want songs written on the edge of the table, not the middle. So, where is the edge? Where is the middle? What does a song at the edge of the table sound like?

I've done some research into the lyrics of the world's top-three songs in all genres, and it's really interesting. Although some genres seem to be filled right now with quite a lot of explicit lyrics, these rankings still demonstrate this weapon — songs at the edge of the table in most genres. For example:

- Queen's "Bohemian Rhapsody." Where did that song come from?[1] For me that would have been well and truly off the edge of the table, but it's worked, clearly.
- Jimmy Webb's "MacArthur Park," nicely sung by Jimmy, Richard Harris, and Donna Summer, but it's pretty at the edge of the table, lyrically.
- The Beatles' "Sgt. Pepper's Lonely Hearts Club Band," another right at the edge lyrically.

Or take the current top three songs in the overall charts in the UK in 2019:

- Lil Nas X, "Old Town Road" (remix feat Billy Ray Cyrus). At the edge of two tables: Country and Hip-hop/Rap.
- Billie Eilish, "Bad Guy." Alternative, space, speech, and right at the edge of production, too ("Duh").
- Lizzo, "Juice." Pop, 1980 samples and speech and shouts, again production edge of the table.

All of these hugely successful songs have something either in the writing of the music or, as often as not, in the lyrics that bring it away from the middle of the table of others who might be writing that kind of genre.

So maybe it's time to ask yourself: do you want to write safe songs that land right in the middle of the table? Or do you want to take a chance on a song on the edge? If you're looking to succeed as a songwriter, it looks like you'll be in pretty good company on the edge.

Summary

In this part of the book, we've looked at why and how to organize ideas and songs, the Song Chain, the Idea Bank, and how to organize fresh ideas, writable ideas, and organized ideas before writing the songs themselves and finishing them to send them off. We learned how all of this information is useful in tracking our work, including demos, cuts, our co-writers, and writing trips. The aim of all of these is to keep the housekeeping as painless as possible to have access to everything, everywhere. We have also looked at the Songwriter's Secret Weapon II: writing at the edge of the table.

In the next part, we will look at the tools of the trade for us, including all things to do with our craft, network, and technology, to help you be creative and ready to be prolific as a songwriter.

Exercise

If you have a copy of *The Organized Songwriter's Workbook*, this would be the right time to take a look at Exercises #5-8.

PART THREE
HOW TO ORGANIZE TOOLS OF THE TRADE

"To be a creative and prolific songwriter.
Even when I don't feel like it."

YOUR BEST INVESTMENT

Everyone has their shopping list. Some things are essential, and some things are nice to have. Whether you are a beginner or a pro, I'm sure your list is very different from mine. Along my journey, though, there was a critical moment that changed my songwriter's shopping list dramatically. That was when my journey took me in a more fruitful direction.

In Part 3, we look at the tools of the trade for the organized songwriter, including all things to do with our craft, network, and technology to help you get ready to be creative and prolific.

What should songwriters invest in?

You might be thinking that I'm about to ask you to get out your checkbook right now. Well, I'm not. I'm REALLY not. Before you buy anything in terms of a new studio, your dream guitar, or a new piano, here's something that happened to me that changed my life — and budget — dramatically.

Just when I was thinking about quitting my corporate day job to become a full-time (still hopelessly un-pro!) songwriter, I needed to figure out what songwriting is all about. So I got myself on a flight to Denver as the only UK registrant at the GMA's "Music in the Rockies," a weeklong festival with a combination of seminars, competitions, concerts, and events related to Contemporary Christian Music. It also covered other genres of Christian music and the Christian music business industry. In other words, it was perfect for my purposes.[1]

Estes Park, Colorado, was a beautiful place up in the mountains with amazing views, wonderful long walks, and slightly thinner air.

But the best thing about the conference was the quality of the seminars. Towards the end of the event was a workshop on Q&A with five well-seasoned songwriters, producers, and publishers. One question asked by an attendee was,

"What should songwriters invest in?"

"Good question," I thought. There were several suggested pieces of equipment to invest limited cash on — a specific plugin, their best guitar, the speakers/monitors for their studio, and a particular specification of computer, for example. But then one of the panelists offered us a piece of solid gold. She said:

"The best thing to invest in your songwriting is not a piece of studio equipment — it's your craft."

SUE C. SMITH

And she was so right. Craft is worth much more than any single piece of equipment or software, which continues to change from one week to another. And I followed her advice. When I look back, the most critical investments in my songwriting have been in my craft: Berklee Music Online, *Write About Jesus*, SongU, Kingdom Songs University, Music on a Mission, Thinkspace Education, and The Rabbit Room. These are all solid gold investments for us songwriters and composers; I highly recommend them. And, in my view, this is the best investment for songwriters.

After the next few chapters, you might find you have a few things to add to your tool shopping list. And, if you're anything like me, you might also have a new set of priorities focusing on your craft rather than on technology.

What are the tools?

Tools are something that helps us get a job done. They are not a substitute for the person doing the job, but something that can help them get it done. Whether you're a beginning songwriter or a pro, there are many tools available to you, some of which are very expensive (a studio) and some are simple and less expensive (choices).

If ideas are where all songs start, spending too much money on our songwriting tools can be the end of our careers as songwriters! From my experience, especially with the huge impact of changes in technology, there are several black holes we can find ourselves getting lost in, and which we need to try to avoid. Just because we don't have everything doesn't mean we need to have it.

There will be some tools we might feel are needed, meaningful, and worth spending the investment; at the same time, there will be some that are not so much needed but just nice to have. According to your budget and timeframe, which category a given tool falls into is very much up to you, but we'll be discussing both types in this section.

Remember those three legs on the table of songwriting? Craft, Networks, and Technology? Let's keep those in mind as we run through how we can be safe, creative, and ready to be productive as a songwriter. Yes, even when we don't feel like it.

CRAFT

These are some of my favorite craft-related tools in my personal tool-box. Put together, these tools make our craft as productive, creative, and fun to work with as possible. In this section, I'm going to simply run through some of the most important tools for my craft, which fall into five broad categories (none of which, you might notice, come with huge price tags):

- A sacred space
- A sacred moment
- Creative habits
- All-weather writing
- Education

Don't worry; after digging into these, we'll move onto tools for the other legs of the songwriting table.

1. A SACRED SPACE

Sure, on our computers we can write anything anywhere. But despite the amazing technology we have in this day and age, there is something special about having your own writing space. Having a place that you associate with creativity and productive work will help you get into that mindset much more easily and reliably, especially when it's filled with objects you find helpful during the task of songwriting.

Your sacred space can look like virtually anything. Here is what I fill my own space with, to give you a few ideas:

1. **A separate physical space** — A separate room where my favorite stuff can be kept.
2. **A comfortable chair** — Actually, I have three chairs! The one I spend the most time with is a big upright wing chair that's been covered to look like where it belongs (in my studio). It's where I'm writing this book right now. Then, there's a reclining cool office chair for my studio desk. I seem to go through one of these every two years! Finally, there's a

leather adjustable piano stool that sits under the grand piano until I get to work. The nice thing is it's always set at just the right level for me. It's a good stool for recording guitars too.

3. **Cool lights** — There are several lights here in my studio. The most important ones are my LED strips that tell me when to start and finish my work: at 8:30 a.m., my LEDs kick on to say "time to work," and I (normally) get straight to work. At 6 p.m., it turns itself off, and that's when I generally go find the family. It's a good routine and it's easy to manage because it's linked to the Wi-Fi. My kids think this makes it the coolest office because it can be in any color, according to my mood or time of the day! I also have a bright light at my writing desk where I can charge my iPhone/iPad.

4. **Candles** — Essential. I've got so many various aromas that my supply will last for a year or so. These candles actually make me think I'm back in Nashville because it always smells nice in the writing rooms at Brentwood Benson/Universal. (Plus, it tells me when Christmas is coming.)

5. **Art** — I'm not really into buying expensive art, but I do have some art my daughter painted at school, and I still love it. The trouble with art is it can affect the acoustics if there's too much glass around.

6. **Quiet** — My studio is a lovely quiet place, which serves two different purposes. First, it's a vocal space, with noise dampers, two doors, and a bass trap, which means I can make whatever noise I want to make. It's important the whole house doesn't hear everything! Also, having such an incredibly quiet place means that I love writing here, in my own space, away from the outside world.

7. **A dedicated writing area** — My desk has space to write by hand as well as several computers and keyboards,

and other instruments, including nice monitors and speakers.

8. **Solitude** — I need my studio to be a private space within my house so I can leave my work around without fear that anyone will take a look, move anything, or tidy up. It's always there when I come back to it, and a safe place to do the best work of my craft. A lock on the door is important for this (especially while homeschooling two young children!).

9. **Sacred objects** — This is important for me: if I'm writing worship songs, I want this place to feel like it's for worship, so I find a small cross and candles make it feel even more sacred than it did before.

10. **A place to play** — I need a space to explore and throw around ideas, no matter how crazy, before I can hone them into something credible and finished.

11. **Favorite instruments** — I keep all my favorite guitars, keyboard, mandolin, and plugins close at hand.

12. **A right-brained, creative space** — This is a dedicated part of my studio that is a fun place to be. This space wakes up the right side of my brain instantly.

13. **A left-brained, logical space** — A separate area that serves as my office. It's where I do business like planning trips, doing courses online, making connections with other creatives using social media, working on my website, and anything to do with the left side of my brain.

14. **A trophy area** — I have a wall and shelf for trophies, certificates, awards, nominations, and even inspiring quotes by important people.

15. **A good background for video calls** — Given people use video more than ever these days, it's important for when I'm video co-writing to make it feel like my partner can be invited into my workspace, even if they're 4,000 miles away.

16. **Inspirational reading material** — From time to time,

I find having something I can hold in my hands to be much more inspirational than reading on my Kindle. On my bookshelf, I find it especially useful to keep notes from courses and workbooks. My favorite book is *Sammy Cahn's Rhyming Dictionary*.

17. **Natural light and air** — I find both of these elements extremely inspiring when it comes to writing time. Since I live by the sea, as soon as the weather gets warmer, I always open the door to get the sea air to fill my space! Natural light is also important, especially in the spring and summer. Winter can be a time when I just close everything up and live in candlelight. I always have a lovely rug close to my writing chair, one that I pull over myself when it's a little cool.

18. **A big cupboard for everything else** — Everything I've detailed so far are the most important things for my own sacred space, but this is by no means an exhaustive list. I have plenty of other items, too — everything that could possibly make my space feel magical, including guitar picks, old studio gear I no longer need, and old keyboards I don't want to sell (yet!). It's important to get rid of anything I don't want to look at, anything that could or would distract me, so I keep it all shut away in a cupboard.

Obviously, I'm not saying you need all the same objects I have; it's just what works well for me, and I think it might work for you, too.

Writing on the road

As special as my studio is to me, it's by no means the only place I write. I've written songs in all sorts of places — my favorite coffee shop (Costa), my favorite sandwich cafe (Pret a Manger), on the train (I co-wrote a lovely song with Sue C. Smith on the 16:36 from

London to Bognor Regis), my favorite chair in our drawing room at home.

In fact, sometimes it's helpful to write in a completely different place. For example, during this season of lockdown, writing this book has been different than my usual writing process. While Costa and Pret may not be great choices for writing in the field these days, I have five places I've been writing around our house:

- At the writing desk in my studio (obviously)
- The multiple screens of my DAW studio desk (helpful)
- At the table in our bedroom, looking at the sea (inspiring)
- In bed (chill)
- My favorite chair in our drawing room (comfortable)

You might find this similar for your songwriting too. Don't be afraid to experiment with different spaces while writing.

Safety

I've always had a studio. It started in my early teens and has come with me everywhere. Even when my corporate life took me to several different countries, my studio always went with me. It wasn't just a studio, but also a notepad of ideas, a tool to produce songs to perform, record, just writing on my own, and entering songs in competitions. Wherever I lived, there has always been a sacred space where I worked on writing and producing songs.

There were seasons and places I remember as very creative. For example, when we rented a lovely big townhouse in Holland — I had the whole top floor as a studio, and it was fantastic. Then there were other seasons that were very dark, like when we lived in Nigeria. Even when Shell, the oil company I was working for, gave us a beautiful big house to live in, most of the studio never got out of the large brown boxes that carried my gear over by boat.

Sure, it was a crazy adventure for us: newly married, no children, both working in Port Harcourt, an amazing culture to explore, amazing dinner parties, our own staff — driver, maid, gardener — and the company gave us a lovely house to live in. But there was one big problem: it did not feel safe. Despite having armed guards patrolling the high-fenced compound (called the "RA" — residential area), from the second I arrived in Nigeria until I finally came home, my creativity was almost dead. There were genuine security reasons, but that's another story. The reality is: unless I feel safe, I never do my best work as a songwriter.

It's worth mentioning that safety is all about *feeling* genuinely safe, not the actual danger of a given situation. If I had known just how dangerous living in Nigeria would have felt, I'd never have agreed to a posting there.

Why am I writing about this?

Life is too short.
And as a creative, you are too valuable to spend life in an unsafe place.

When security is a genuine issue, then sure, capture the experiences in your journal, but unless you feel particularly inspired or motivated to write, don't worry about using the experiences with your craft until you are in a place you can thrive. Unless you have a special calling on your life to be in an unsafe place, move! You are way too valuable to spend a moment on this. Be in a safe place, because that's when your craft is going to come out to play, dance, and grow into something special.

I'll say it again: Life is too short. And as a creative, you are too valuable to spend life in an unsafe place.

2. A SACRED MOMENT

It sounds funny to think about time as a tool, but it is. One of my co-write friends, Gina Boe, told me about her routine a few years ago. At one point, she had a full-time job, and four kids homeschooled, and she still found time each week (Thursday evenings) that was her sacred moment for writing songs. She's now a Dove award winner with #1 songs in various genres, and that would never have happened without keeping her sacred moments. I still use her "sacred moment" idea to help with my own writing.

By "sacred moment," I mean a special time set aside exclusively for songwriting. It doesn't have to be a great deal of time, but it should be regular and uninterrupted — social engagements, chores, phone calls, and anything else will have to wait. The moment is only sacred if you give it an ultimate priority.

Here are some ideas you might use for your sacred moment:

1. **Save it in your calendar** — It doesn't need to be Thursday evenings; it can be any time, any day, or days. I'm

grateful to be able to use most of my days in my studio now, but it never used to be like that until I made it happen.

2. **Guard that time jealously** — It's important to have some kind of agreement, especially if you are working around family. Without that, there will always be another thing you will be dragged into. Guard this time jealously.

3. **Give your right brain some quality time** — Being a songwriter doesn't mean you have to spend every second of your sacred moment writing. Listening to other music, reading, taking in inspiring films — this can all help. But they have to be all about writing a song at the end of it.

4. **Fill the well** — Every now and then, it's helpful to take a break from your writing to see the world from different eyes. Sometimes you need to get out there to take in the world and fill your creative well. Take a walk along the beach, view some art (either at an art gallery or online), read poetry, consume some theatre or literature. There's always a title there somewhere.

5. **Set a time for creative habits**— I'll be talking about this in the next section, but it's important to create a moment that makes it happen. For me, first thing in the morning is best for creative pursuits like writing.

6. **Schedule everything** — This may seem odd, but, for me, blocking parts of my calendar for writing is essential. This is partly because there are a million other things that would stop me from writing songs (or anything) — work time, family time, chores, social time, you name it! So what do I do? I schedule all of those things, too, as best I can. While my family is incredibly supportive of me as a writer, there are a million other things that we could do as well, so blocking time with the family is the best way for the family to help you block time for writing.

3. CREATIVE HABITS

At the end of the day, your songwriting muscles are also tools, and tools need to be sharpened just as muscles need to be exercised. As such, it's necessary to keep those creative muscles in shape even when you're not writing.

There are many different kinds of creative habits that I've found along my journey, but here are several I'd recommend as regular practice:

1. **Object writing** — This was the first time I did any kind of creative habit after reading *Pat Pattison's book, Writing Better Lyrics*. The idea, basically, is to pick an arbitrary object — a real object — and to describe it with as much sensory detail as possible. This is set out in Chapter 1 of his book, and Pat's methodology is awesome. I'd totally recommend it.

2. **Destination writing** — This is an incredibly helpful application of Pat's methodology I found in *Andrea Stolpe's excellent book Popular Lyric Writing — 10 Steps to Effective*

Storytelling. Andrea is also another teacher of songwriting and talks about this in detail in Chapter 2 of her book. In short, it's sense-bound free writing focusing on a place, a person, or a time instead of an object. Similarly, you need to write describing everything related to the senses of touch, taste, smell, sight, sound, and movement.

3. **Morning pages** — This was something I found in Julia Cameron's *The Artist's Way Workbook*, which I found incredibly helpful. It was a time when I had quit my corporate job but still felt too left-brained and not right-brained enough. Well, that book introduced me to a new way of looking at creativity, and morning pages are right at the heart of her work. Brilliant stuff.

4. **Journaling** —I use journaling to write about what's been going on in my life, how I feel about it, and what I'm going to try to achieve in my day ahead. And sometimes include my creative to-do list. It's a good way to get the day kick-started. It's also a great way to put on paper what you feel about things going on in your life, especially bad moments but also good moments as well.

5. **Free writing** — That is one of my favorite creative exercises because, well, there really are NO RULES. Except for one: to write more than 500 words and/or write for 15 minutes. I'd say that out of the 20 years I've been songwriting, 70% of my creative habit time has been spent on free writing. I love the freedom of free writing. It's the best way to exercise your writing muscle — just like you might do at a gym — especially if you combine some of these other methodologies. Squibler.io is a nice place to have fun. Obviously, if a cool idea for a song lyric or title arises, I capture these every time.

6. **Blogging** — I love blogging. While I don't use it as often as I used to, writing for an audience is a great habit to be in. Knowing that someone was likely to be looking at my blog

(even if only one person was out there) is a great way to
capture shareable ideas whenever they arrive. I find I write
better for a blog than when free writing. Capturing blog
ideas is very similar to capturing new song ideas.

7. **Free playing** — This is my musical equivalent of free
   writing. When I started really enjoying my time free
   writing, I realized I was missing the opportunity to exercise
   my musical muscles. So I started a similar thing — just
   jumping on the piano each day for 15 minutes and playing
   anything. Often a great musical idea will just pop out. And,
   of course, I capture everything that's worth keeping.

8. **Practicing** — It may sound strange but spending some
   time on your chosen instrument a) makes you a better
   musician, b) takes you to different places from a songwriting
   perspective, and c) opens up a new set of skills that you
   might actually use during writing, recording a work tape, or
   even in demoing.

There are a number of different creative habits I looked at, but these
are the most potent that have helped me as a songwriter. If you've not
used any of these, I'd suggest you give them a try.

4. ALL-WEATHER WRITING

All-weather writing is not one of those tools you can buy. It's a mind-set, a choice, a decision to be the kind of songwriter described in the first part of this book. If you want to be an organized, successful song-writer, you'll need to decide to be an all-weather writer. Here's what I mean:

Going beyond the routine and preferred space and time described above, many writers will only write under certain circumstances. For example, they may decide not to write unless they have:

- A certain brand of coffee drunk from a certain mug
- Sunshine
- A seat facing the right direction
- A certain candle smelling a certain way
- No paperwork needing to be done
- Dishes and other chores finished

Believe it or not, they are all REAL hurdles people have said they needed to overcome before starting to write songs. And you may have your own hurdles. When I first started my new job as a songwriter, I had my own, too — for me, it was the weather. Yes, unless the weather was lovely, I would tell myself,

"Surely, I can't write the best song without the sun shining today."

The trouble is, any hurdles are bad for your writing. This kind of hurdle is the worst because you're putting it there yourself. So finally, when I decided to be an all-weather songwriter, I started doing my work like I did when I was doing a corporate job — out of my house at 6:30 a.m. and writing when I got to my studio. No matter the weather, I do my job during work hours.

Now, it's important to understand the distinction between having a sacred space/moment as described above and putting hurdles in your way. Set yourself up for success by giving yourself the tools you need, by all means. But make sure you aren't making those tools an obstacle; you don't want to stop yourself from writing before you start.

Here are a few guidelines for all-weather writing:

1. Write, write, write — When I sit down to write, I just focus on one single thing: writing. And just carry on writing. And then again, until I've finished a draft. Use a timer here if needed pomofocus.io

2. Write what is exciting to write — Every time I sit down to write, I look through my Idea Bank to find what writable ideas I'm excited about. Nine times out of ten, it turns out to be one with a high "Cool" score. Being excited about what I'm working on helps get from idea to draft.

4. Filter out no-hopers — In my last book, I talked about the idea of the spectrum of writability. When you're writing, you'll want to spend your time focusing on the top 60% of writable ideas and filter out the no-hopers. Here's a picture of what I mean:

Spectrum of Writability

5. **Don't write, rewrite** — I remember from my life as an equity analyst in investment banking, I used to start with a simple idea behind a product and work on it and work on it until it was good enough to send out to clients. The approach was to keep working on it until it had become the best product it could be. It's the same thing with songwriting: sure, I can keep hacking away until I've written a great finished draft. But, especially when I'm writing on my own, I always go back to it to make it as best it can be. I have song drafts number version 70 and more to make sure it's the best it can be. So don't neglect other works in progress in your all-weather writing!

6. **Timing** — This is another lesson from my corporate life: start work when the office is open (for me, it was 6 a.m.) and finish when you've done your work (for me, 5 p.m.). Do I work 11 hours a day in my sacred space? Well... yes, sometimes. These days it's rare, but I certainly used to when I started as a songwriter. I'm not saying everyone needs to spend that long on their writing. But I did.

An all-weather writing day

One of the lovely readers of my last book asked me what a pro song-writer's day looks like. In reality, there is no fixed agenda or deadline except the quota. Everyone has their own schedule, and I tend to keep fairly regular hours when home in my own studio. But when co-writing in Nashville, here's what my days look like:

- **5 a.m.** — Devotions and journaling. At the start of the week, I always wake up early because I'm still on UK time (a six-hour difference). This gradually gets later and later as the week goes on!
- **6 a.m.** — Preparing for my co-writes. This involves asking the what, who, where, when, why questions that go in the "trips" part of my Idea Bank.
- **8 a.m.** — Breakfast.
- **9 a.m.** — Travel to the co-writing venue.
- **10 a.m.** — My first co-writing starts. It's mostly chitchat for the first 15-20 minutes, and then ask the question, "What shall we write today?"
- **12:30 p.m.** — Lunch, with or without my co-writer(s). Sometimes over lunch, we might get back to the writing room to finish the draft and work tape.
- **2 p.m.** — Second co-write. Same way as above, but afternoons are generally a little less productive, so we wrap up around five or 5:30. I'm not saying the product is not as good (they might actually be better due to being more chilled out), but it's just a different feeling.
- **6 p.m.** — Early dinner.
- **7 p.m.** — Third co-write, if it's an evening co-write. This is a somewhat rare occurrence, but it's the same deal as above. If I'm not co-writing in the evening, then I chill out, update my Idea Bank (SIF, lyric sheets, work tape delivered to publisher and co-writer).
- **9–10 p.m.** — Bed!

It sounds crazy busy, and it is. At the end of a trip like this, it's great to get back home to have a few days off. When our children were a lot younger, there was less opportunity to take time off, but it's still great to have time with the family again. "Jet lag" is not a phrase we use in our household!

I know it sounds like a lot of work, but as songwriters, we do work, and that means all-weather work. If you want to be a full-time songwriter, you need to be ready to work in all kinds of conditions and settings; otherwise, it's just a hobby.

5. EDUCATION

This is our own continuing professional education (CPE) — another import from my corporate life (see Part 2) on Songwriter Competencies. CPE is basically the ongoing training that is required to remain a certified professional in that field. You may well have yawned at that last sentence (I did!). Don't worry; there's no such thing as a certified songwriter, thankfully!

Instead of worrying about certification, let's start thinking about the onion.

How big is your onion?

Many years ago, when I finally left my day job to become a full-time songwriter, I realized a truth about myself:

The more I knew, the more I knew how much I didn't know.

It was fun, but, to be honest, a little scarier than I was expecting. It's a little like when I first started driving. I remember as a child, I used to watch my father driving, and he made it look so easy, safe, and secure. But when I started driving myself, it wasn't quite as simple as I thought.

Well, being a full-time songwriter was also way more difficult than I'd thought. So, just like I needed a course of driving lessons, I had to go back to school to learn how to write songs properly.

The onion

Sure, before I left my day job, there were many years I'd already enjoyed the incredible interplay of harmony, melody, bass, and rhythm. Becoming a songwriter was one of the most wonderful journeys ever. But for me, there was another journey I needed to embark on: lyrics. And becoming a full-time songwriter, I had to figure out how to write lyrics. This was the onion.

What's all this about onions? Well, when I started on Day 1 of my songwriting career, I thought I needed to learn the skills about the size of an onion, one I could hold in my hand.

Right now, though, as I look at the size of the world of songwriting, it's the size of a giant onion I can't even get my arms around. And I continue to learn more things every time I co-write with my brilliant co-writing friends.

Even now, it's humbling when I still realize how much I don't know about my craft, but it's lovely to still be on a journey. And I am beginning to think that the journey is actually better than reaching the destination.

OK, OK, so let's get into it. Why onions? How is songwriting like an onion? Maybe this next picture captures this better...

1. There are many layers to learning how to write songs. Just when you feel like you've found the top layer and learned everything there is to know about songwriting, you find another, more significant layer out there. Each book I consume or course I finish, I discover yet another layer that I need to understand.

2. Sometimes, when you get to the core of your writing, it can be a tearful process to find out what you are writing about. Just like cutting up an onion!

3. For me, songwriting has given my life so much greater richness. Imagine how bland life would be without songs! (Imagine how bland life would be like without onions!)

So here's the question for you — how big is your onion? If it still fits in your hand and you don't have all that many layers under your belt, it's probably a good idea to seek out some further CPE to help you move forward.

My own CPE

As should be clear by now, there is still a wealth of resources out there that can keep you moving forward in your journey as a songwriter.

Here are a few ideas I've used:

- **Berklee Music Online** — I can't recommend this highly enough. At one point, I'd finished all of Berklee's 12-week songwriting courses, starting those with Pat Pattison's three main courses: "Lyric Writing: Tools and Strategies," "Lyric Writing: Writing From the Title," and "Lyric Writing: Writing Lyrics to Music." All three of Pat's courses were amazing, especially taken together with his books that were very helpful. If you'd already done these three, I'd totally suggest the course "Commercial Songwriting Techniques" by Andrea Stolpe and the cool course by Jimmy Kachulis, "Songwriting: Writing Hit Songs." There is lots of Berklee Music Online for free here at coursera.com that's worth taking a look at.
- **SongU** — This is something I learned a lot from, and it's well worth looking at. These are less expensive than Berklee but still brilliant content. The thing I love about SongU is that its founder, Sara Light, was able to get access to much of Sheila Davis' amazing content. That's golden stuff.
- **Write About Jesus** — Another amazing resource, again much less expensive than Berklee. It's obviously more related to Christian music, and it's historically been held once a year in October. I owe so much to Sue C. Smith, who is the founder of WAJ. If you are a worship writer, CCM, or SOGO, there are more than a million reasons out there for you. The faculty is spectacular, and you'll get the opportunity to meet everyone over the meals and the competition, which is so cool. You also hear their work at the Friday evening "writer in the round," which is a highlight for my year each year. Check it out.

I mentioned several other sources at the front of Part 3. For example, Kingdom Songs University, Music on a Mission, Thinkspace Education[1] and The Rabbit Room[2]. As I said, they are all great sources for CPE, and there are others out there. They all exist to help us develop on the journey, becoming better and better songwriters than we'd ever have thought we could be.

So, if those are the craft-related tools, what's out there for networks and technology? Well...

Craft

Tool	Essential	Nice to have
Sacred space	Safety, quiet, space for writing, playing	Studio, office, double doors, lock
Sacred moment	Blocked, agreed, time, quality	Guarded time, filling the well, a set 'work time'
Creative habits	Free writing, journalling	Blogging, other
All-weather	Inspired writing, rewriting, filtered ideas	Write, write, write, certain times that work best, financial
Education	WAJ (Christian), SongU, others, key books	Berklee Music, other sources

NETWORKS

I've always used a three-legged approach to my work, whatever it is: craft, networks, and technology. And when I quit my day job, I realized just how much I needed networks more than ever. Here's why:

You can write the best song on this planet, but without a network, no one will hear it.

That's why we need networks. And as songwriters, there are several key networks you need to maintain:

1. Family
2. Co-writers
3. Creative friends
4. Publishers, and
5. Critics

Each group needs to be managed. So, how do we manage them?

1. FAMILY

From my point of view, the family is always #1. The world is so much better, whatever I do when I've got the support of my family behind me. And I suspect it's exactly the same for most songwriters. Here are a few ideas that might help do right by your family and help them do right by you:

1. **Keep the family happy** — If I'm looking to write the best song ever, how are my head and heart going to get me in the right place if I am not OK with my family? There was one co-write I had with a friend of mine whose 16-year-old son wasn't happy with the idea of us writing. At one point, he actually set my co-writer's guitar on fire. Honestly! This should be a memorable illustration of how it's not just important but critical to managing your family's needs!

2. **Share your work when you're ready** — Try to keep your work in your own space until you're sure it's time to share it. It's not about being secretive, just a little protective. This may well depend on the amount of musical experience that's in your family, but sometimes sharing an idea or a

draft lyric to anybody, including family, can sometimes either push it somewhere it shouldn't be or even strangle it before it's given a chance to breathe. Better to share a bit later than too soon, that's my view.

3. **Ask the family for ideas** — This might seem like the total opposite of #2. But, depending on kind of family you are, it might work to help you figure out where a song could go. My wife, Sandra, is actually a brilliant songwriter and has many song ideas I use. There have been moments when I'm preparing to co-write online, and she comes up with ideas when I ask for them. And it's free!

4. **Block out songwriting in the family calendar** — We have a single calendar we have access to as a family. We have family time together most meals (especially during this pandemic lockdown) and evenings together. This is a special time. So, if I am writing or recording something in the studio during that special time, I make it clear to communicate the change and expectations appropriately.

5. **Explain your songwriting goals** — Songwriting is, to be honest, unusual for most people. Your family may love music but have no idea just how deeply you feel about your work. Especially if you have (or are about to) quit your day job! But when you make that move or are even just taking it a little more seriously, if you explain your reasons, it's going to be easier to spend all that time in your studio.

6. **Be sensible about your songwriting finances** — Finances can be one of the biggest issues among family members. Everyone has their own plan and financial demands. Sometimes my wife has more sense than I do when a new plugin or midi controller comes to the market. Make sure a new tool is in the budget before making a purchase. And if it isn't, waiting another month or even longer isn't going to trash your goals. (Plus, by then, there may be an even better version on the market.)

7. **Pray about it** — As a Christian family, we often pray about all sorts of things, especially my work. If I'm co-writing, making a trip to Nashville, or even working with the Worship Team at our Church, it's great to have them behind me in prayer.

One way or another, songwriting has to fit with the family somehow. Not reconciling your songwriting with your family is a shortcut to a short career.

2. CO-WRITERS

I talked about co-writing a little in my last book on Song Maps and said that co-writing has been one of the most wonderful surprises of my songwriting journey. It's true, and I'd still say that today. Regarding the way to approach co-writing, I also said:

"DO WHATEVER YOU CAN DO TO BEST SERVE YOUR CO-WRITER. "

It's about doing your best to be your best. But what does it mean to "best serve your co-writer?" Here's what I keep in mind when co-writing:

1. **Focus on writing the best possible song** — As a more grown-up songwriter, I'm able to offer different strengths to my co-writers than I used to. For example, I now know more about my relative strengths in writing lyrics and music versus the strengths of most of my co-writers.

Most great writers will focus on writing the best song rather than focusing on who does what.

2. **Try to leave your nerves outside the writing room** — I remember once, early on in my co-writing career, I was all churned up before a co-write with an amazing writer whom I'd looked up to for years. To make matters worse for my nerves, they'd just won a Dove Award the night before for their part in an incredible song. When they arrived, the first thing I did was congratulate them. And their response was, "So this is when you find out I'm actually a fraud," which was their way of saying that they felt almost as nervous and vulnerable writing with me as I was feeling writing with them. In other words, nerves are normal but unproductive. Deal with them before getting into the room, if at all possible.

3. **Come to your co-writes with great ideas** — This is the time to work your Idea Bank and, in particular, have already figured out several (ideally three to five) writable ideas. Be ready to pitch the idea to your co-writer to the point that they REALLY want to write that idea.

4. **Spend time to see their ideas** — Even though I work hard to come to my co-writes with the best ideas I can, it's important that I'm honest when my co-writer has actually come with an even better idea or an idea they clearly want to write. It's important to give just as much energy to their ideas as your own!

5. **Never hold back your best ideas** — This is something Pat Pattison said to me once, and I'm paraphrasing it: never hold back the writable ideas at the top of the list in your Idea Bank. You might have penciled it in for your next co-writer, but that individual might not be destined for it. These ideas have been sent to you for a reason, so be your best co-writer and use them right now

where you are, not save them for the future. There will always be new ideas later.

6. **Be happy to shut up** — Sometimes, I find my co-writer has hit a rich vein of inspiration. The worst thing in this situation would be for me to try and make the song go somewhere else. If my co-writer has struck gold, it's best to help them capture that, every time.

7. **Enjoy the silence** — Sometimes, co-writing is about giving each other enough time to process the ideas you're talking about. Sometimes it's about contributing just the odd line or even just a phrase or word. That's fine. One of my co-writers (who I know is reading this right now) is a genius lyricist. She is able to take our idea and disappear into her world with her computer and come back holding a diamond. I love co-writing with her!

8. **Try to finish the song** — Yes, try to finish the song. *Expect* to finish the song. It's not the end of the world if it's not finished, and it's always possible to rewrite it. But, given a chance to sit in the same room with someone for two to three hours, it's always great to have a finished product as a goal. The last time I went to co-write in Nashville, I wrote with two other (amazing) co-writers, and we went home with three finished and demoed songs. That's always a great way to finish a trip.

9. **Don't be a word counter** — This has never happened to me, but I know there are a few out there. The best co-writers I've worked with have always split the royalties into the normal shares (i.e., 100% divided by the number of people in the room). If I were a word counter (100% divided by the number of words contributed by each individual), I don't think I'd be asked to co-write again! Keep your eye on the big picture rather than the paycheck: you want to have a long-term working relationship with your co-writers, and

ideas come from all of us, whoever came up with an
individual word.

10. **Be a good hang** — Sounds odd, but I have had co-writes
that just didn't work. It's rare, but it's almost always
necessary to have the vibes for a good hang. After all, life is
too short, and most songwriters would sooner co-write with
someone who's fun to be with than someone they can't
stand!

There are so many more tools and tips for co-writing; I'll be talking
about this more in Part 4.

3. CREATIVE FRIENDS

Creative friends can be all sorts of people — producers, artists, worship leaders, musicians in bands, other songwriters. Whoever they are, you're looking for lovely people who understand how your brain is wired. But it's not just those who are involved in the music industry (broadly) who are great to have around. Some other individuals who can be helpful include:

- Media people
- Designers
- Web people
- Painters
- Sculptors
- Creative entrepreneurs

The list is unending of people who could help you on your journey as songwriters. My best creative friends were actually friends I made at courses and seminars — largely producers and artists — who ended up being co-writers, too.

But we're talking about tools of the trade. How can these people help us on our journey? Here are some ideas, based on how they've been helpful for me:

1. **Connections to connections** — While doing one of the Berklee Music Online courses, I happened to find myself in a course with a producer based in Nashville. Later, I set up a time to meet up at his studio when I was on one of my writing trips in town. He happened to be producing an A-class artist, who's husband is an incredible producer and musician. This led to all sorts of other great writing opportunities. My friend at Berklee was a great connection to other connections.

2. **Teacher friends** — On my journey as a songwriter, I've met all sorts of people on the way, many of whom have expert knowledge in some other competencies around songwriting. I've met incredible artists, producers, guitarists, piano players, pastors, worship leaders, Bible teachers, authors, speakers, online teachers, and the list goes on. And every one of these individuals had something to teach me. When you meet someone with expert knowledge, even without asking to be taught anything, you can quickly absorb so much new information that you would never otherwise acquire any other way. Just be receptive to learning when that happens.

3. **Understand their wiring** — Creative friends often have brains that are wired differently than most people's. I remember one particular friend of mine who was teaching songwriting at the same conference as I was. He has an incredible ability to come up with the perfect lyric lines. After chatting with him and having a chance to co-write together, I suddenly realized what he was doing and how his brain was wired to constantly get these lines right. In my

own way, I started doing exactly the same thing in my writing. This is not (yet) in a book. But it works!

4. **Industry know-how** — Chatting with music types, whether you are writing with them or not, you'll end up talking sooner or later about what's happening in the industry. These are golden opportunities to capture information on all sorts of things you'll never find in a book or a course. It also shapes your own journey and writing more clearly.

5. **Gear** — By gear, I mean technology for my studio. Remember, technology is one leg of the table, and that starts with getting the right kit in your studio. So many people I chatted with over lunch or coffee gave me amazing ideas about how to upgrade my studio to be Nashville standard sounds with inexpensive solutions or helped me learn the difference between essential gear rather than nice to have gear. Without spending time with these people, I'd never have gotten close to the right gear in my own studio.

Creative friends are, in my view, one of the most important secrets to networking. If you hear of someone you think might be key to helping you along your journey, take notes, approach tentatively, wait until you see them in person, then find a way to chat, and then ask your questions. You might actually be the right person to help them on their own journey, too.

4. PUBLISHERS

Publishers are less easy to find. But if they know who you are, it's a whole load easier. For many years I used to send tracks (CDs and lyric sheets) to publishers unsolicited because that's all I knew to do. Eventually, I learned that nine times out of ten, my work never got close to a publisher to hear unless they already knew me. The best ways I think to connect with publishers are:

1. **Find out who's who** — When I was looking for a publisher, the first thing was to figure out who is who in the industry. The person you're reaching out to could be just a gatekeeper (junior executives) or the actual publisher at the companies (creative director). Find out who is the real decision-maker. Once you know that, go about finding anybody, anyplace who can offer a way to get to see them IN PERSON. Unfortunately, there are quite a few people out there, depending on genre, so you'll need to do your homework.

2. **Use conferences as marketing opportunities** — Conferences are incredibly helpful. On the one hand, they

enabled me to acquire knowledge about what publishers were looking for. But after moving my craft closer to what I knew publishers would be interested in, that's when I switched from student to marketing role. Marketing is all about making sure publishers heard my best work, in competitions, in one-to-one sessions, song critiques, and everywhere to make sure they heard my songs. That is what conferences were all about.

3. **Find out why you want to see a publisher** — This is an odd thing to say here, but in reality, the world of music publishing has changed and is continuing to change very fast. The reason I needed a publisher was that they already knew where to pitch my songs. They are part of the village. These days, some of that community still exists, but it's more limited by genre and industry. You need to know why a publisher is needed to move you forward on your journey before you reach out to one.

Why you might need a publisher:

- To pitch your songs and ultimately get them cut
- To help set up your legal details and PRO, and learn how all that works
- To connect you with other pro songwriters to co-write
- To set up co-writing with artists
- To encourage your quota (mine was 12 equity songs per year at Universal)
- To collect royalties and pay your share to you

On the other hand, there are many reasons you might not need a publisher. For example, if you want:

- To manage your own contacts and co-writes yourself
- To manage your own songwriting output (your own quota)

- To own your growing catalog and freedom as to what happens to it
- 100% of your equity share of all songs you write yourself or in co-writing
- To manage your career in a more hands-on way

From my experience, my publisher was invaluable in developing my career in the first few years of being a full-time songwriter. Having said that, the creative director (Holly Ward) I worked with was an exceptional publisher. In short, a publisher can be helpful when starting out, but whether you need to continue to have a publisher looking after you when you've established yourself is dependent on where you want to go with your career.

5. CRITICS

Critics can be anyone, from your mom (who would probably love all of your work) to press (who will either love or hate your songs) to people who critique your songs at conferences (e.g., WAJ) or online services (TAXI, Nashville Songwriters International, Nashville Christian Songwriters). And more besides (maybe the congregation at your church!).

So how can we use these individuals as tools for our songwriting? You may well think I have a negative attitude towards critics because this is my main advice to you:

"Don't take them TOO seriously."

The reality is that all critiques are subjective views, not the gospel. Some critics might rightly point out issues that will be a problem for other listeners as well. But still, don't take them too seriously.

The only exception I would make would be people with full-time songwriting people or publishers who are critiquing your work face to face. This is because when you see someone who's a pro, you can see in their face and body language how they process your song and the emotional impact of your lyrics and music.

This type of critic is also more likely to suggest specific changes from an informed perspective. And even then, after experiencing the critique itself, put it away for a few days and then look at it again in the light of a fresh day. Then, at that point, when it all makes sense, try a rewrite of the song again.

Networks

Tool	Essential	Nice to have
Family	Happiness, prayer, goals, finances	Family calendar, ideas, share
Co-writers	Best song, great ideas, silence, never hold back	Listener, nerves, try to finish
Creative friends	Understand their wiring, connections	Teacher friends, knowhow, gear
Publishers	Who's who, why, connections	Conferences are marketing opportunities
Critiques	Don't take too seriously	Publishers, family

TECHNOLOGY

So now we turn to technology. This is certainly one of my favorite subjects; I could honestly talk about technology for a very long time because it's taken me a long time to acquire the right gear for my studio. And of course, technology changes quickly and, sometimes, dramatically.

A lesson from the corporates

During my corporate career, I worked for the oil company Shell International. While Shell is a massive company (with over 120,000 employees at that time), there was something great about working for Shell. It was well organized, carefully managed (almost too much, sometimes), and incredibly well funded. The internal mantra was:

"If you want to be the best, you need to have the best people, strong funding, and the best tools and technology in the market."

There were many risks involved in getting oil out of the ground: geological, commercial, political, financial, and more. So there were enough risks there without using anything other than the best tools.

Well, it's the same thing for us in songwriting. If you think about it, there is a long list of risks involved, from idea through to recognition. At every step of the process — creative, commercial, production, marketing, finance, relationships — you are taking a risk by putting your song out there. While I stand by what I said about there being several black holes money can be thrown into, it is important to increase our chances of success as songwriters by mitigating those risks.

So, how do we decide what technology to spend our money on? Here's my view:

Get the best possible tools you can afford within your budget.

Whenever I bought a cheap version of anything for my studio, it was just a question of time before I had to go back and get the more expensive piece of equipment. And that genuinely set me back in doing the best job I could do.

Let's face it: this business is competitive, incredibly competitive. And if you jeopardize your own successes as a songwriter, then someone else (a competitor) will snap up that success first. That's a tough thing to say, but it is the truth. If we haven't invested in the best tools of our trade to help us on our journey, the risk of getting songs cut is affected. Sometimes terminally.

So, how is technology able to help us be more productive as songwriters? There are several opportunities for using technology, both in terms of hardware and software. You can invest in:

1. Tools for capturing ideas
2. Tools for building an Idea Bank
3. Tools for writing lyrics
4. Tools for recording music
5. Tools for connecting

Let's run through those categories one by one.

1. TOOLS FOR CAPTURING IDEAS

As mentioned earlier in this book, capturing an idea is the first step in writing a song, and the goal for me is to capture every idea I come across, wherever and whenever it arrives.

Tools for capturing ideas can be as creative as you like, and either low- or high-tech.

Theoretically, I would honestly suggest you use ANY way you can to capture the idea. I've used all sorts of tools in the past:

- I've scribbled ideas on the back of a flyer for my brother's business.
- I wrote a lyric on a steamy bathroom mirror after a shower then took a photo of it with my phone.
- I've written many ideas on old Church service notes.
- Receipts are great, especially if they are blank on the back.
- I've captured music on cassettes, voice memos, emails, and voicemails.

Having experimented with many different systems, here's a breakdown of the tools I use to capture ideas now:

- **Paper** — Any kind of paper with a space to capture an idea is great, especially for capturing lyric ideas. But of course, it needs to be kept safely—ideally filed in the Idea Box I mentioned earlier in the book, so it can be reviewed and worked on. It is critical that these are sent to my Idea Bank; otherwise, it's easily lost or forgotten. I have two scanners to process this paper Idea Box to get in electronic files: a single bed scanner, which is good to use for oddly-shaped pieces of paper, and A multiple-page scanner, which is great for batch scans.
- **Sending a voicemail to myself** — Only used in an emergency, but if I'm in the car, I will give it a go. The nice thing about this is given my car is now Bluetooth-enabled, I can call myself with a song idea while driving. Cool.
- **iPhone Music Memos** — My favorite musical capture app! I only found this by accident, but it's the music version of Apple's Voice Memo app. It's amazing because it even does its own drums and bass and makes it available to be imported (with all of your files) within GarageBand and Logic. iPhone Voice Memos is also great for both lyrical and musical ideas.
- **Apple Notes** — This is brilliant for capturing lyrical ideas. I've used a million other apps — Evernote, Notability, iA Writer, Scrivener, Ulysses, Google Docs, Word, etc. — but Apple Notes is as good as anything.

Either way, the key to capturing ideas is this: they need to be held somewhere safe so they can be processed later and added into the Idea Bank. Once in the Idea Bank, they can be used as a writable idea later, turning a few words or lines into a writeable song.

2. TOOLS FOR BUILDING AN IDEA BANK

Having captured fresh ideas in your Idea Bank, this is a great tool for working these into writable ideas, such as using a Song Map.

There are many different ways of building your own Idea Bank. To keep it as easy as possible, your Idea Bank could be kept simply in one big document or a spreadsheet. I've used a number of different ways of doing this over time, including:

- A simple list in a spreadsheet, such as Google Sheets
- A relational database such as FileMaker Pro
- Alternative apps that are also worth looking at, like Notion

In my last book, *Song Maps — A New System to Write Your Best Lyrics,* I mentioned a way to create your own Idea Bank using spreadsheets. Let's review a few concrete steps for doing that now.

How to build an Idea Bank in a spreadsheet

Step 1: Create a spreadsheet — This is ideally a Google sheet or an Excel spreadsheet. Name the first sheet, "Idea Bank," and the second sheet, "Co-writers." In the first "Idea Bank" sheet, enter the following:

a) In Row 1, Column 1, enter the title "Idea Bank" in bold.

b) In Row 3, enter the titles across the sheet as follows:

- Reference number
- Date
- Title
- Link to Lyrics
- Link to Music
- Song Map
- Status
- Cool Score
- Genre
- Structure
- Tempo
- Possible Co-writer
- My share

In a second sheet, "Co-writers," enter the following:

c) In Row 1, Column 1, enter the title "Co-writers" in bold.

d) In Row 3, enter the titles across the sheet as follows:

- Name
- Publisher details
- PRO

Step 2: Enter your data: Fill in as much as you can with all of your ideas and co-writers. For example, if on April 24th you captured an idea for a slow country ballad, a story song about saying goodbye to a dying dog, enter each of those facts in your first empty row — at this point, you would have something entered under Date, Genre, Song Map, Tempo, and Status (Captured, for now). And a Cool score (try not to score all at 10/10!). As you work on this idea a bit more, you'll add more info to this row and update its Status accordingly (i.e., Writable, Organized, Written, or Delivered.

Step 3: Celebrate! You are now probably more organized than most of your fellow songwriters!

The benefits of this option are that it's simple, it's easily managed, and all that's needed is your favorite spreadsheet. Plus, there are plenty of free spreadsheets like Google Sheets that need very little in the way of technical skills. And it's fun!

The downside of having this on a simple spreadsheet is that it's a 2D database, which means certain data might need entering more than once. But, actually, I love the simplicity of this.

In order to set this up, here is a Google Sheets template https://tinyurl.com/Idea-Bank that you can copy/paste and use on your own drive.

How to build an Idea Bank in a relational database

When I started to get bogged down on my admin work with all of my ideas, songs, quotas, co-writer details, etc., I decided to take on another learning curve to be able to write my own relational database. I chose FileMaker Pro, which was an Apple product at that stage (now part of Claris).

FileMaker Pro

FileMaker Pro is a little more grown-up than some of their former sibling Apple products like Bento, but not so complicated that you need to have a Masters in Computing and Programming. This app does everything I want:

- It's genuinely relational, so it helps to define complex relationships between key data.
- You only need a single entry for all data.
- Automating is simple in order to keep homework fast and painless.
- It works on OSX, iOS, and even PCs.
- It has great security.

I must admit, I've been really happy having gone through the investment in time to learn FileMaker Pro. Apart from everything else, at the end of a busy day of writing in Nashville, even with three songs written in one day, I can have all my Song Information Forms (SIFs), work tapes, and lyric sheets sent out at the press of a few buttons. And as with other Idea Bank tools, it lets me access everything everywhere.

FileMaker Pro is so helpful that I wish I could give it away to all my lovely readers! I could go on about its benefits, but I know I could spend more time plugging this application than writing this book! All I can say is: if you have an appetite for spending the time to learn a relational database program, I would totally recommend it. It's a great competency that has been helpful, though it's not an essential skill for writing great songs.

Notion

There are many apps out there that I've been looking over to find a perfect tool for songwriting, but only one always comes back to me: **Notion**. This is a relatively new boy to the market (versus FileMaker Pro) but, if you have an educational email address, it's FREE! And apart from that, it's actually a very smart app, halfway between spreadsheets (2D databases) and traditional relational (3D) databases, plus it's easier to learn than FileMaker Pro.

Again, if you have an appetite for learning Notion, I'd also recommend that. Here's a link to it.

www.notion.so/product

Notion is a flexible database that allows you to change it in any way you need. The lovely thing about it is that you only need to enter data such as co-writers' details once, and it becomes available to any other views you are working on. Cool stuff.

And here's what both FileMaker Pro and Notion looks like from my iPad (although it works on many platforms):

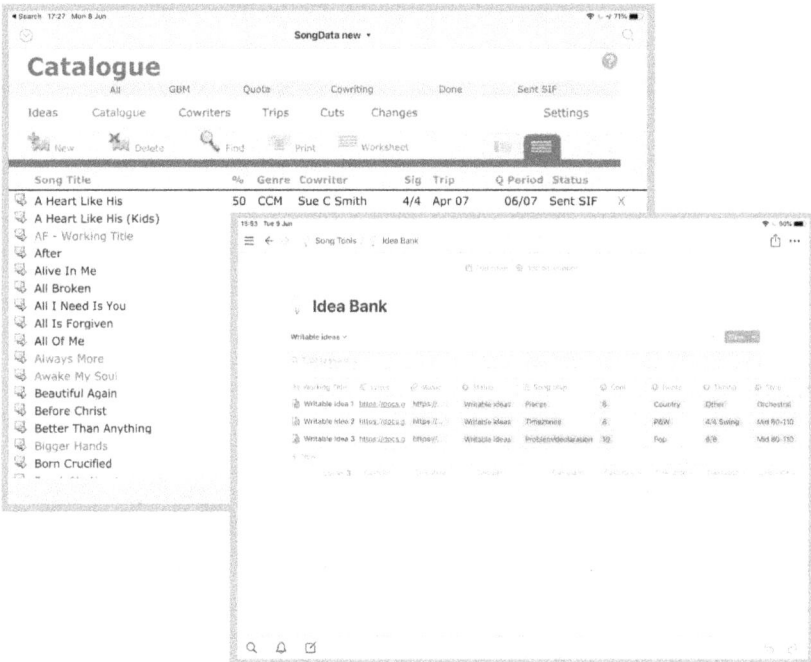

Captured ideas in FileMaker Pro and Notion

Having captured all the ideas as writable ideas, the Idea Bank is also a great place to take them to the next step: Organized.

This is simply reviewing writable ideas and deciding things like who, when, where the idea could possibly be written — either as a co-write or on your own. The thing that makes this organized is being planned to actually turn into a written song, the next thing we need tools for.

3. TOOLS FOR WRITING LYRICS

Writing the lyrics is, of course, one of the most important parts of songwriting.

Again, there's a lot of physical gear as well as software, so you can easily spend a lot of money on this. Let's look at hardware first.

Hardware

The corporate world still runs on Windows, so that was what I tried to use at the beginning of my songwriting career. After three years of trying to make my PC laptop work for songwriting, I finally had to do what all of my co-writers did and buy my first ever Mac, primarily to co-write over video. That was the beginning of 15 years of loving everything Apple. So here's what I use now:

- **MacBook Pro** — I have one of the top-of-the-line laptops with a silent 2 T SSD of storage, and it was so worth spending the money on that. Without this computer, I couldn't do what I can do now. It's not just because it's incredibly fast (which it is), but because it's both the center of my writing as well as the center of my studio. So it comes with me everywhere around the house.

- **MacBook Air** — This is not really used as a laptop because I've set it up to be a desk machine as my office workstation. If something important or serious needs to be done, it gets done on this.
- **iPad Pro** — This is what I use on my writing trips, especially going to the US. Having bought a Brydge keyboard, this tablet is the best of both worlds —able to type on any apps I have at the same time as being incredibly light and mobile.
- **iPhone X** — By now, this model is a little old, but the last time I went to Nashville to write, we wrote three songs in one day, all on my iPhone. I have my Idea Bank both here and on my iPad (using the FileMaker Go app), as well as a few other apps that are really helpful.

Software

I love trying different apps for both OS X and iOS. The most important apps I've been using are:

- **Word and Google Docs** — I have a similar template for lyric sheets and music. The thing is, I love having these resources available with me everywhere. I've used iCloud, Google Drive, Dropbox, and OneDrive, and they all work well. Google Docs is particularly good for video co-writing because everyone can work off the same document. Everyone still uses Word, but Google is probably better for me.
- **FileMaker** — As mentioned above. This is where my Idea

Bank is held as well as a few other apps I write with. Before FileMaker, I used **Excel** and **Google Sheets**. These are key to writing lyrics, finding ideas, and other tasks.

- **Finder** — All of my songwriting files are in eight folders on my MacBook: Cuts, Demos, Lyrical ideas, Lyrics (i.e., finished), Musical ideas, SIFs, Working files (FileMaker files), and Work Tapes. I am religious about keeping things in the right place. Of course, this can be done in Google Drive or anywhere like this.

- **rhymebrain.com** and **rhymezone.com** — These are great websites for rhyming ideas. The trick is to prioritize the meaning of the lyric above the rhyme. Understanding family rhyming from Pat Pattison in his book *Essential Guide to Rhyming* was an important journey for me.

- **Evernote** — This is something I've used for a long time now. It's very much my "second brain" for storing anything in it. Everything is in there: flight details, initial ideas before logging in my Idea Bank, WAJ talks, and anything else you can imagine. It's particularly great to be able to automatically set up my Fuji bulk scanner files to send to Evernote. It just works.

4. TOOLS FOR RECORDING MUSIC

I love the fact that recording is an art as well as a science. Recording a final draft — a work tape — is a great way of remembering what it's supposed to sound like, even if the final song track sounds rather different.

This is important because if you spend the same amount of time on a work tape as you would on a demo or the actual cut, you might well miss a lot of the creative ideas captured during the writing. It doesn't mean that more time can't be put into a song later, but the work tape is supposed to capture all that's been written rather than represent a finished track.

This is the final part of any songwriting, whether on your own or a co-write: recording the work tape and sending it to your publisher (even if you are your own publisher).

To give you some idea about my setup, here is a photo from my studio.

So, what tools do I use for recording?

Hardware

For work tapes, I always use my iPhone (the Voice Memo app), like most of my co-writers. Then I send the file to myself and to my co-writers by email if they haven't recorded it. It's simple. But what about in my studio?

- **Main computer: MacBook Pro** — As I said above, the MacBook Pro is at the center of my studio, linked to a million things. It's a MacBook Pro 16 GB DDR3, 2.6 GHz Intel Core i7. I also have a second computer, a Windows with 12 GB ROM, 2 TB slave, that I mostly use for samples.
- **Storage: 2 SSD drives** — I have two Samsung 2T drives. They are amazing, silent, secure, and for samples, it's almost like they are inside my Mac. I'm not sure what I'd do without them!
- **A backup computer** — My MacBook Air laptop in the office is also my choice of mobile tracking if needed and is a backup if the main computer falls apart (which it hasn't yet, thankfully).

- **Keys: Yamaha C3 Silent grand piano** — This is both a real piano and a quality midi keyboard. It's one of my best friends and links into the studio from the other side of the room. There are a lot of songs in that piano. I have a few other keyboards kicking around, but they are nothing like playing on a grand piano.
- **Guitars: McPherson, Larrivée, Fender Strat acoustic/electronic** — These are all the instruments that I love working with. Everyone needs to find the best one for themselves. I actually have two Larrivée guitars, one at home and one in Nashville. Back when I was traveling so much, I was fed up with having my guitar bashed up so many times by airport baggage handlers I found it easier to just keep one in my destination.
- **Monitors: Genelec 8010A + 7060 Active Subwoofer** — It's taken a while, but I've finally ended up with something perfect. It's not the same sound as a boom box, but it gives me a clear audio sound. Important.
- **Interface: Prism Sound Orpheus** — It's been with me a few years now, but it's an amazing interface — the ADA converters are used at Abbey Road, so needless to say, it works fine for me.
- **Mics: Neumann U87, KMS 105, twin KM 104** — These work so well in the studio. I've had various mics along the way (Audio Technica, Studio, Studio Projects), but in the end, my journey ended with Neumann.
- **Out of the box: Avalon Vt737sp, UA 1176LN** — Along with ADA coverts as well as a booth constructed bass trap + sE Electronics Reflexion, this completes my vocal/acoustic journey.
- **Midi controllers** — I've tried several, but right now, I'm using two: Nektar Panorama P1 and an Icon Platform M+. They are both fine. Each has its own quirks!

There are a million different places where you can find out more about what gear is needed for setting up your studio, from the bedroom to pro studio. For me, Sound on Sound is the best source.

Software

In terms of software, everyone also has their own favorite. When it comes to DAW (Digital Audio Workstations), VSTi, FX, and mixing, there's no written answer to what you HAVE to have; it's just what kind of music you're composing and recording. Here's what I use:

- **DAW** — This is a bit like asking someone's religion, but I use Logic Pro X more and more. I also have Cubase 10.5, which I've used as my main DAW for many, many years. I also have ProTools and Reason.
- **Studio plugins for FX and VSTi** — I have most iZotope, Native-Instruments (Kontakt), Output, Spitfire, Sonokinetic, Cinematic, LA scoring 2, Vir2, Tooltrack, Waves, Spectrasonics, Nord Stage 3 sampled, Yamaha CFX Concert Grand, and many others. This is why I have all that hardware storage! Right now, I love Spitfire for composing and Native-Instruments Noire for a piano. Lovely.
- **Mixing and Mastering** — This is getting into some of the black art of mastering, but I love iZotope — especially the latest versions of Ozone, RX, Neutron (more mixing), and Nectar (more vocals). I also use Finalizer from TC Electronic; it's really well thought-out technology. But I also use online mastering if I just want to give it to someone else to hear with new ears. I've used Abbey Road a lot in the past, but it's expensive. I currently love CloudBounce, which allows me to master as many as I want for a year. That works for me!

With all of these options, there is no set answer to what you need. These are the tools I use, my gear, and rooted in my approach to technology, but it's certainly not the gospel on this subject — it's just what works best for me.

5. TOOLS FOR CONNECTING

Over the pandemic crisis, we've all found ways of connecting with the people we need to see and speak to. The three I've used are:

1. Zoom
2. Facebook Messenger
3. WhatsApp

But when it comes to co-writing, which we're covering in a bit more detail in the next part of this book, what tools can be used to make it work better?

Here are a few suggestions I'd make:

1. Smartphones now have amazing cameras, especially an iPhone (or a similar-quality Samsung).
2. When participating in a video co-write, place the camera slightly above eye level. Don't hold it too low, or viewers will be looking up at your chin or up your nose! Similarly, don't

hold it too high, or they'll be looking down from great heights.

3. Look at the camera, rather than at yourself.
4. Hold your camera in landscape orientation, not portrait.
5. People should see you in a video call, not your stuff. Get your clutter out of the frame (that includes your bed).
6. Think about getting a tripod. I use a tripod attached to a mic stand, and that works well. It's so much better to have the camera stabilized.
7. Take some time to create the best lighting for your video co-write. This doesn't have to cost a lot of money; after all, it's free to capture the video in natural light.

Technology

Tool	Essential	Nice to have
Capturing	Something to capture an idea	Paper, apps
Idea Bank	Paper, spreadsheet	FileMaker Pro, Notion
Writing lyrics	Something to write, Word or Google Docs	Laptop or iPad
Recording music	Something to record, smartphone	Studio, DAW, gear
Connecting	Good internet, Zoom/Messenger	Stage your set

Essentials and Nice-to-Haves

We've looked at a lot of different tools for songwriting across the three legs of craft, networks, and technology, but let's return to the big question for you: what should you invest in?

My suggestion for anyone reading this book is to think hard before you spend any more money on tools for songwriting. Not because you shouldn't buy tools—you should! But before buying, you need to give yourself some time to figure out which of these two categories, a given tool falls into. Is that shiny new tool...

- Essential?
- Or nice to have?

In Appendix E, I've set out my top-20 essential things needed for me as a songwriter. But that's only my view! Some of the things I've talked about in this book are not even strictly necessary, including a studio. Yes, not everyone needs a studio! If you are a lyricist more than a musician, you may well not even want to have a guitar or piano. Your journey is not the same as my journey.

But if I had to recommend what goes on the Essentials list first, I'd suggest prioritizing these:

1. Safety. Make sure you feel able to be creative wherever you are.
2. Your sacred space. Pick somewhere special to you.
3. Your sacred moments. Choose a time you'll look forward to writing.
4. A creative habit you love. Maybe try something new?
5. Your network of creative friends and co-writers.
6. Your own Idea Bank, in whatever form you need to capture fresh ideas, writable ideas, your lyrics, music, work tapes, networks, and your catalog.

7. Some basic technology. After all, you need something to capture all of your songs, but exactly what will work for you will depend on budget, preferences, etc. Just invest in what works for you.

It's entirely possible that even after carefully selecting only what gear is necessary, you'll still end up with a lot of stuff. But remember, the more competencies you build as a songwriter, the more likely you will need to have sufficient gear to work from home.

Summary

In this part of the book, we looked at how to organize our tools of the trade, to help to be creative, and get ready to be prolific songwriters. We've looked at the tools for our craft, network, and technology to give us the best chance of being successful, including the Idea Bank, our own space, and more. By now, you should have a good idea of what tools you'll need to start looking at to get your songwriting journey off the ground.

In the next part, we will focus on how to organize our co-writing, including how to best serve and nurture co-writers, what 'writing up' is, etiquette, timing, arriving having prepared for your co-writes, with your best writable ideas, how to co-write with artists and a whole lot more.

Exercise

If you have a copy of *The Organized Songwriter Workbook*, this would be a good time to take a look at Exercise #9-11.

PART FOUR

HOW TO ORGANIZE CO-WRITING

"To best serve my co-writers, so we write the best song."

SERVING YOUR CO-WRITER

Co-writing is genuinely a brilliant way of songwriting. When two different, creative minds combine ideas, skills, approaches, and suggestions into one song, math laws fall apart — two plus two always equals way more than four.

In this part, we will focus on how to organize our co-writing, including how to best serve and nurture co-writers, "writing up," etiquette, timing, arriving having prepared for your co-writes with your best writable ideas, how to co-write with artists, and a whole lot more.

In my last book, I said that co-writing has been one of the most wonderful surprises of my songwriting journey and explained how critical it has become for me. Not just for my development as a writer, but for the quality of songs I would write. I also didn't realize how many great friends I'd make along the way.

This is still very much true for me today, and there is probably another book I'd love to write about the whole subject. But this book is about organizing, so let's look at how to organize ourselves to make co-writing work best for us and, maybe even more importantly, to serve our co-writers.

Every one of the co-writers on my list is a special person in my view:

- All have differently-wired brains.
- All are prepared to take a risk.
- All can make something beautiful together rather than just on their own.
- All enjoy spending three hours with someone else to make something new, commercial, and of creative value.

These are people we need to nurture, just like the ideas we all bring into our co-write sessions, and we are mostly very different people coming to create a new song together. At the end of the session, the song will be better if we best serve each other.

Serving our co-writers

So, how can we organize ourselves to best serve our co-writers? There are five major ways we can accomplish that:

1. Be in the right place.
2. Arrive on time and well prepared.
3. Just make it work.
4. Understand that co-writing means writing together.
5. Prepare for writing with artists.

In many ways, this is about preparing, so on the day of the co-write, we can walk in knowing that the session is going to work. And not just be an OK co-write, but a brilliant co-write that will, hopefully, lead to another co-write together. Let's get to it!

1. BEING IN THE RIGHT PLACE

I'm not talking about location — before you leave the house or fire up your video chat software for a co-write, you need to make sure you're in a good place mentally.

Being in the right place in our heads is all about preparing, and that happens way before the co-write starts. It's about being the right person for our co-writer to meet.

- Not the person who has a million things on their mind other than writing.
- Not the person who is worried about other things going on.
- Not the person who is more concerned about what a hundred other people might need from them.
- Not even the person who is nervous about meeting their incredible co-writer.

It's all about...

The room, our co-writers, and the song.

Nothing else.

Yes, nothing else. And that means on the day of the co-write, we are focusing on that and that alone.

I remember the first time I ever co-wrote a song. It was a tough time for me, but it was also tough for my co-writer because it was the first time for him, too. He was a fantastic guitar player and also a great lyricist. My worry at the time was how on earth I could come up with anything to help him write a better song! The fact is, while he certainly had some great ideas, having a second brain and a different perspective was still incredibly helpful. In fact, one of our songs got published by a major music publisher a little later.

Would that have happened without the co-write? No. Both of us being in the right place made that work. Here's what that means from an organizational standpoint.

Imagination

Before you set out to go to your co-write, take a moment to think about what exactly that session is going to look like. Close your eyes and imagine what it will look like in the co-write, what it will feel like being there on the day, and how it is likely to sound. Then, think about what it will feel like to have finished an amazing co-write with a great song created. Think about what has happened to achieve that.

That's the mental preparation that will guide your preparation for this co-write, especially when you're writing up.

What is writing up?

Writing up is when you are co-writing with someone who is more experienced than you are at co-writing songs. That will always be the case when you start co-writing. The more you co-write, the less you'll be writing up. But, in the beginning, it's an inescapable reality.

Is it a bad thing if people realize you are writing up? The short answer is no — writing up is an incredible opportunity to learn a lot more about co-writing and songwriting in general. Writing up enables you to learn way more about the craft than can be found in all the books and courses out there. So, my view is: accept it, enjoy it, and make the most of that special moment. It's all part of the journey.

Etiquette

Etiquette for co-writing is important. It's not like there's a rulebook out there; it's all about feelings and soft skills. But it's still important, especially if you have not yet had your first ever co-write.

So here's my view on co-writing etiquette[1]:

1. **Respect** — This is my #1 unspoken rule of co-writing. Whatever your co-writer says, whether they're giving sucky ideas or brilliant ideas, always treat your co-writer with respect. Assume that they are always trying to do their best with the song, even if you suspect they are not.
2. **Jobs** — There are many jobs incorporated in the songwriting process (I'll go into this more later in the book). Work out what job your co-writer would like to do, then you do the rest, especially if you're writing up. And be flexible about the song being written; otherwise, some cool ideas could be missed.
3. **Positivity** — Being positive is about supporting your co-writer, even when they are still figuring out the right words, phrases, melodies, hooks, or chords. With that in mind, remember that there is always a positive way to deliver a negative response — like "Sounds great, but what if we did

X," or "Let's use that and maybe come back to it again later." Maybes and what-ifs are great ways to achieve this.

4. **Alternatives** — Your co-writer might be a fantastic lyricist, but one of the reasons for co-writing with them is to provide a different perspective, to help them see something that they wouldn't be able to notice without you being there. So, even if they are an amazing lyricist, it's a mistake to give up on your own contribution. You may well deliver the best idea for the song.

5. **Arrive with great ideas** — I've talked about the tools for co-writing above but, in reality, there are two reasons to arrive with great ideas at a co-write: First, whether I'm co-writing at my own studio or I'm on the way to Nashville, knowing that I've got 500 ideas, many of which are totally writable ideas, lets me look forward to the co-write rather than be worried about it. Second, even if we end up co-writing someone else's idea, it's important to be able to deliver the best idea for your co-writer, and that takes some preparation. This is especially true if you are writing up.

6. **Focus on ideas, not processes** — This is something Pat Pattison said to me about co-writing when he came to London. When you are co-writing, focus the discussion not on how to write songs but on the song itself. In other words, focus on IDEAS, not the process of how to turn these ideas into songs. In reality, everyone has their own process, and they need to turn the ideas into a great song, not be lectured on the right way to accomplish that.

7. **Never hold back** — I mentioned this earlier in this book, but when you're in the writing room, if you're looking to find a great idea to write, then get out the best possible idea you have whoever you're writing with. Even if you're writing up in your next co-write session, you might be working with the best writer for this idea right now. So don't hold back your best ideas.

8. **Dare to suck** — This is something one of my last co-writers mentioned a long time ago, but it still works now more than ever. What he meant was, whatever idea you think might work for a line, a phrase, or a verse, even if it sounds a little silly, ALWAYS share it with your co-writer. The thing is, even if it seems a dumb idea for the song, it could well encourage your co-writer to come up with a better idea to articulate it, and they wouldn't have thought of it without the silly idea you came up with. That's why I don't like counting words for sharing the percentage of a song; daring to suck will always make the song better, even if it's not precisely included in the final song. Being able to suck is part of being a better co-writer.

9. **The room is the room** — I can't count the number of times I've been in a co-write, and one of my co-writers asked me, "Can I say something that will stay in the room?" Of course, that's an unwritten rule for all of us co-writing people anyway: whatever we say, whether it's a sucky comment or a brilliant one, everything stays in the writing room itself, and is not discussed outside. That's part of keeping the relationship in the writing room confident, and it enables a deeper set of ideas to be written.

10. **The door is the door** — The same thing goes for stuff outside of the writing room: our focus is to write the best song we can in the time we have together. Anything that could come in the way of that — life issues, egos, financial issues, relationships outside of the room — all have to be left at the door before coming into the writing room. Being in the right place in our head means being able to leave things outside the room, with the door shut.

2. RIGHT PLACE, ON TIME, WELL PREPARED

This may seem an obvious suggestion, but you'd be surprised how often I encounter songwriters who don't manage to put it into practice. The reality is, people are busy — sometimes crazy busy. But no matter how busy I am, I make sure to take the time to be super-organized when I travel to Nashville. After all, how stupid it would be for me to travel 4,000 miles and to not turn up to the right place and on time? After 18 years of co-writing in Nashville, I have never done that once. That's a critical part of being an organized co-writer.

Value the details

To make sure I end up just when and where I need to be, I always set up my schedule with all the details, including:

- Who
- When
- Where (e.g., my place, their studio)
- How long it takes to travel

And, is it a FIRM date? Or is it a POSSIBLE co-write? There is a difference!

This is pretty much all I can do to make sure I show up prepared. But what happens if I make it to the room and one of my co-writers doesn't turn up? In my view, there are two options for how to deal with this:

- **Option 1** — Chalk it up as a misunderstanding (the first time it happens).
- **Option 2** — Expect it to happen again (if it's happened more than twice).

So if we get to Option 2, does that mean I would never have a co-write with that writer again? No, because they are still a great writer, and I always want to make time to work with a great writer, especially if I'm writing up. However, I wouldn't generally fill my schedule with them more than once during one trip. If I'm not careful, I could end up coming all the way over from here to Nashville without having co-written at all!

The power of coincidences

It's funny, but once, when I was waiting for a co-writer who didn't turn up, I decided to stay in the writing room booked for me to prepare for my next co-writer later on that day. And what happened was amazing.

Coincidentally, the exact thing happened to the writer next door to me, so we decided to co-write instead. And he was an A-class artist whom I'd never imagined I'd have a chance to write with. That's the power of coincidences. It just goes to show that God has a better idea of my schedule than I do.

Well prepared for your co-writer

I mentioned the idea of matching ideas to co-writes and the importance of transforming basic, fresh ideas into writable ideas. Whenever I'm on a trip to Nashville, I always have my Idea Bank packed full of ideas, but I also have selected at least 5-10 writable ideas that are ready to write with a specific co-writer. This is a key part of getting prepared for a trip.

In this process of preparing, here's a few key questions pertaining to your specific co-writer that you might find helpful:

- What do they love writing most?
- What genre would they want to write?
- What is their strength, lyrics, or music?
- What's their journey as a writer?
- Where might they want to go next on their writing journey?
- What else do they do outside of writing? Worship? Bartend? Friday live evenings?
- Are they into technology?
- What's their publishing situation?
- Where might they want to go further with their writing journey?
- What other songs have they cut so far?
- If they are an artist, what style of songs would they be looking for help to write?

Hundreds of ideas could potentially work with your co-writer. But if you arrive with a little more information about your co-writer in mind, you will know what ideas in your Idea Bank will be best for them. This preparation is incredibly helpful, but it takes time.

3. JUST MAKE IT WORK

Once you make it into the room at the right time, prepared and ready to go, the next step is all about maximizing the time co-writing, which means minimizing the introductory chit-chat and get writing. In reality, it's great to catch up with each other; we all love that. But everyone is there to write, so let's write!

I have one co-writer who is always a little bit late, but as soon as she arrives, we get cracking writing. Normally she comes with a "pre-written" lyric, which helps us write a complete song really quickly. It's a dream writing together: I always love her lyrics, and she loves my music. Plus, she's always hilarious to work with.

The lovely thing about co-writing is there are no rules, just tools. Our joint success is purely based on the quality of the song that comes out the other end of the co-write. And anything can happen in the writing room. But here are a few general suggestions to make your co-write work better:

1. **Smile** — If you've never met your co-writer, say hi and make them feel welcome!

2. **Explain** — Explain more about who you are, saying what you do and what kind of music you're working on

3. **Fast intro** — It's obvious to say this, but the faster the intro you have with your co-writer, the quicker you get writing, so keep it as punchy as possible. Try and keep your introduction to 15–20 minutes or less, if at all possible.

4. **Money** — If you've not written together, I would say something about money, right upfront. If you're looking for a phrase that works for me, I say, "Normally we split the royalties 50–50. Is that OK with you?" (Or whatever equal division works for however many people are in the room.)

5. **The Question** — If your co-writer hasn't said it yet, once the conversation is gently moving towards co-writing a specific song idea, that's your opportunity to ask The Question: "So, what would you like us to write?"

6. **Three Big Ideas** — Normally, the above question would naturally be answered with them, introducing an idea — a title, a lyric, or a musical idea. If not, this is when you introduce your own ideas, ideally writable ideas that you've already prepared and seen what their response might be. If you have prepared properly, you'll be prepared to pitch (yes, pitch as in gently trying to sell) an idea they'd love.

7. **Take their ideas above yours** — If they *REALLY* want to write a specific idea of their own, I would generally be OK to give that a go, especially when writing up. At the end of the day, you need to write something, and if they are really into their idea, they should have an idea of how it could work well. After 45 minutes in a co-write, it's time to be writing rather than talking about what should be written.

Once those steps are finished, and you've gotten to the writing, there's a lot of silence as everyone writes their part, and the craft begins in its own magical way.

Things to ask your co-writer

If you've done your homework, you've already prepared for your session with a specific co-writer, even if you've never worked with them before. When you finally meet your co-writer, you'll have a chance to figure out so much more about them. All your assumptions and questions about them will suddenly become answered, often in surprising ways. If you don't already know the answers to these questions, be sure to ask them during the co-write:

- Where are they on their journey as a writer?
- What genres do they really want to write more of?
- Where are they with their publishing?
- What are their current publishing details (to include in the SIF)?
- Where should work tapes/demos be sent to?
- How can you best get in touch with them to set up a follow-up co-write?

These questions will help you organize yourself even better next time you work together. If they love writing songs about kids, let's prepare some ideas between co-writes. If there's a certain idea or genre they want to try, maybe this is something for later. If an artist is looking for something specific, what might be a great idea to write by video next time? Take the time to make sure you have everything you need to know about them.

4. CO-WRITING = WRITING TOGETHER

This is at the heart of us being able to serve our co-writers. In reality, there is always a different dynamic with different co-writers. And we all have our own approach to everything.

In general, though, when you're in the room together, there are three options when two writers sit to write:

1. Two writers writing different songs
2. One writer writing and the other just watching
3. Two writers writing one song together

Here's the hard truth: Options 1 and 2 are not co-writing. Option 3 is. Co-writing is when we collaborate to create a finished song, one that's better than if we had written it on our own. And this must be your expectation at the start of the co-write; otherwise, there's no point, really.

Remember, the point of co-writing — of spending all that time making sure you bring into the room all your best ideas, creativity, skills, charm, and fun, of figuring out how each writer can best contribute to the mix — is all for one simple goal: to make the best possible song.

So, when several people have to work together to accomplish a task, how do they do it? In this important way, songwriting is pretty similar to any other job. Co-writers can work together on the same task, or they can end up doing different jobs within the team.

The fact that there are two or three (or more!) people in the room means that there are two models for co-writing:

1. A partnership, in which each writer takes a turn in the driver's seat.
2. A board meeting (if there are more than two in the room), in which individual writers can have specific tasks or roles assigned to them.

The first of these are fairly straightforward, so let's examine the second in a bit more detail.

Different jobs

As always happens when people organize themselves, there will likely be a certain hierarchy according to what emerges in the room. That means certain jobs will start getting assigned within the co-write.

There are several jobs needed in a co-write, including:

1. **An idea person** — Someone who can bring writable ideas, who takes a cool title and shows how it moves through the song. It can also be someone with chorus ideas, musical motifs, musical or lyrical hooks, last line phrases, or payoffs: the more ideas, the better. In reality, as the co-write settles down, this is a job that bounces around the room to

different people until an "I'd LOVE to write THAT" moment arrives.

2. **A lyric person** — Someone who carries the main lyrical load, though this person is not by any means doing 100% of the lyric writing themselves. I have a number of co-writers who are really strong lyricists. They tend to disappear in their thoughts on their laptops before coming back with a suggested idea, which is normally pure gold. But they also always value feedback, help, alternatives, or inspiration from others to make sure it's getting close to what everyone wants to write.

3. **A music person** — Again, this doesn't mean only one musical idea is done by one person; everyone in the co-write needs to be happy with it. If, for some reason, it's not quite there, then the music person will normally bring back more options. Music, for me, is always there.

4. **A commercial person** — There are several commercial jobs here: someone who can hear the song being cut, for example or someone who knows contacts, publishers, and artists/groups that are out there looking for songs. This person can also potentially nudge the co-write to a new place if it needs to be more commercial.

5. **A timekeeper** — Someone who can keep an eye on the clock to make sure the co-write is as productive as possible. Again, there are no rules, but it's always great to come away with a finished song, and sometimes that means having someone on hand to keep things on track.

6. **A coach** — Someone to help, encourage, suggest alternative options if it needs to be steered somewhere else, and even tell the room if it's still not quite where it needs to be yet. This is one of the most important jobs needed in a co-write.

7. **A listener** — Someone who allows other co-writers to just speak through where they can see the lyric or melody going.

Sometimes one of the most valuable jobs as a co-writer is saying absolutely nothing and just letting it flow from the other co-writer. It's important to know when to shut up. Really.

8. **A secretary** — Someone needs to keep track of the important information and eventually send the song info, lyric sheet, and track to all co-writers and publishers (if appropriate).

9. **A coffee runner** — It might seem odd, but sometimes the best ideas arrive when one of the co-writers is moving around, whether off to get coffee or go to the bathroom.

In my co-writing career, I've had every one of these jobs at one time or another. And, to be honest, I love each of these jobs.

Additionally, don't neglect the perspective brought in by other jobs and careers altogether. Since I've been co-writing, I've been able to import skills from several different jobs I've been employed outside of songwriting, such as being an analyst, an accountant, a company secretary, a chairman, an author, an executive coach, a worship team player, and yes, a coffee maker. All of these came to the fore at different co-writes. These are things others wouldn't be able to do otherwise, and it's great to contribute something unique to the room.

Not writing on my own

This is an important point, so I wanted to make it again. In a co-write, I often think I have a better idea for the song to be written — a musical direction or a lyrical hook, for instance. If, for some reason, my co-writer can't quite see where it fits, or they have better ideas themselves, that's fine.

I'm not writing this on my own; it's a co-write. And both of us need to be happy with the final song.

If we do move in a direction I hadn't anticipated, I always capture all my own ideas that don't end up getting used in a song — I don't capture my co-writer's unused ideas, just mine (that would be unfair). But whatever job I'm doing, whether I'm a lyric person or a musical person, I'm still writing together with my co-writer, not on my own. And my ideas not used in a co-written song are there for me to use in a later co-write instead.

Permission

Sometimes, it's possible that the idea brought to the co-write has somehow turned into something quite different from what you'd imagined. When that happens, you may find that you want to save that unused original material for another rewrite. If so, it's important to get permission from your other co-writer first.

- You could ask for permission to use the idea in another co-write (it would have to be a very different song, though).
- You could ask permission to include another co-writer in this song because you think they might take it to a new level (or know of opportunities, artists, etc.).
- You could simply ask permission to work on it on your own to take it to a new place and send it back to see if that works for them after.

These are all options. But the important point is that you communicate your ideas and preferences to your co-writer so you can get their permission. Permission is all about respecting your co-writer, which is key.

5. CO-WRITING WITH ARTISTS

When I was first signed to Universal, my creative director was great at fixing people I'd be best co-written with. Most of my first few trips were with other staff writers until, after a few trips, it was the right time to co-write with an artist.

It was great fun finally writing with an artist, but it was very different. Certainly very different from writing with other staff songwriters. Here's why:

1. **250 times a year** — Artists aren't just looking to write a good song; they're looking to write something that they can sing in next year's gigs. For some artists, that means 250 concerts a year or more. Needless to say, the finished product has to be something exciting enough to perform 250 times without feeling like it's time to give it a miss.

2. **Edge of the table** — By definition, artists at a co-write are looking for something they can't write on their own. This is why I mentioned The Songwriter's Secret Weapons II. They are looking for something that is on the edge of the

table (but not off the table entirely), something that is different from what other writers, producers, and management can write (yes, there may be people on their team who write songs, too).

3. **Deeper, more meaningful** — Songs written with an artist need to be somehow taking the artist a little deeper than normally. The final product needs to be something that's still part of their own lives but said in a different way. You're looking for something that's generally deeper than they would normally write on their own.

4. **Cooler** — Artists like to encounter a subject or a phrase that they wouldn't have thought of. This is just the kind of thing your Idea Bank could have for them, especially when it comes to writable ideas.

5. **More lyrics than music, sometimes** — If they are an artist/writer, they are often better at writing music than lyrics. This might not be the case, but if it is, then it's time to put on the lyricist hat. It's also possible that you're bringing strong musical ideas, too. That's fine; as with all co-writes, it's all about getting the best song from the co-write, whoever suggests it.

Of course, writing with an artist has a significant upside: if they LOVE the song, there's more chance of the song getting cut on their project. That still doesn't make it a 100% sure thing, of course; the artist may not be empowered to make the ultimate decision (they could have to consult their producer, manager, etc.). But in general, writing with an artist often gives your song an inside track to being included on a project.

This is why writing with an artist is different than writing with another commercial songwriter; your role is sometimes way larger than you might normally expect. You have your job as a songwriter, sure, but you also might be called on to act as consultant, coach, emotional crutch, psychologist, or anything else they might want you to be. Artists are, at the end of the day, still normal human beings with human problems that also try to keep them outside the room. And sometimes those problems might not stay outside. With that in mind, being a friend is one of the most important jobs you have as a co-writer, especially when you're writing with an artist.

Summary

In this part of the book, we focused on how to organize co-writing, how to best serve and nurture our co-writers, how to arrive having prepared for your co-writes, with your best writable ideas, how the dynamic of the co-write can be different for each co-writer (co-writing, not my-writing), and finally how to co-write with artists.

In the next part, we will take this further, how to organize the next steps of our journey as songwriters, including focusing on the journey over the destination, what success means to us, when is it ok to be unhappy, the Song Funnel and what it looks like and how to manage this, and how important it is to get the right balance between our work as songwriters and the rest of life. This has been key for me as a songwriter.

Exercise

If you have a copy of *The Organized Songwriter Workbook*, this would be an excellent time to complete Exercise #12-14.

PART FIVE

HOW TO ORGANIZE THE NEXT STEPS

"To focus on the journey, not just on the destination."

THE JOURNEY AND SUCCESS

This part of the book is all about focusing on the next steps of your journey as songwriters and how to organize that. I'll talk about the importance of figuring out what success really means to us, how to deal with when we feel unhappy with our journey as writers, the concept of the Song Funnel, why so many songs don't get cut, how to manage this, and how important it is to get the right balance between our work as songwriters and the rest of life. This has been key for me as a songwriter.

It's All About the Journey

My time as a songwriter has genuinely been one of the most beautiful journeys of my life. In fact, it's been several journeys – music and lyrics together – and sometimes each on its own. Sometimes it felt like finally climbing to the top of one huge hill before realizing yet another even bigger hill I needed to climb. And then another. And then yet another. And then the hills became mountains. Even right now, I'm still looking at another peak ahead of myself.

The truth of the matter is, intimidating though it may sound:

The mountains don't get any smaller.

I remember when I first started playing the piano when I was just six years old. I discovered my very first notes: middle C, and all the white notes that go with her. Then two notes that sounded cool playing them together. Then three notes, then chords. That was such a wonderful moment! Then I found different keys, G, F, then finding the black keys, and my favorite note on the piano, F#!

Then I stumbled upon melody, harmony, rhythm, and realized how a bass note could change everything.

Somehow, these were some of my favorite journeys to experience. Part of me wishes I could discover this all over again because it was so much fun. But that wasn't where it ended. Dissonance, stability, and repose. Tension and response. And more.

Lyrics were my next favorite journey — titles, development, rhyme schemes, structure, meter, point of view, then other things like prosody, scansion, setting, simplicity, universality, viewpoints, voice, work peaks and troughs, and many other tools to use writing lyrics. And then, Song Mapping! These were all incredible opportunities to grow as a songwriter and to become more and more professional in the craft. There are things out there that I'm still learning about, and I continue to love the journey.

The fact that I'd love to relearn all of this all over again is exactly like the words of Arthur Ashe Jr., the professional tennis player who won three Grand Slam singles:

"Success is a journey, not a destination. The doing is often more important than the outcome."

My point is this: in many ways, traveling along the road actually changes us as human beings, mostly to be better people. We become experts in our own field and better at doing our own craft. This is maybe why the journey really is more important than the goal itself.

Success

But even if you enjoy the journey, you need to ask yourself a very important question before you take one more step:

What, exactly, does success look like for you?

For songwriters, success could mean a million different pictures:

- A tear from a loved one at hearing a song you wrote
- Seeing a handful of people loving your song at church
- Watching your song on YouTube
- Having your song critiqued for the first time, no matter how painful it feels
- Entering a song in a competition
- Playing a song to a publisher
- Your first-ever co-write
- Getting signed as a songwriter
- The first time a song is *professionally* demoed
- The first time you co-write with an A-class artist
- The first time a song of yours is nominated for an award
- Winning a GRAMMY

These are not necessarily milestones for every songwriter; just different pictures of success. Everyone is at a different point in their journey, and everyone's journey ends up somewhere different. As a creative person, it's important not to be told by anyone what success *should* look like — your success is what works for you. The journey is all about enjoying the freedom to define our own success. And my own definition of success is almost certainly not what would work for you or any of my co-writers.

When should we be unhappy?

When I was at the top of my former career in investment banking, there was an exciting moment when I was working as Managing Director, managing an incredibly successful team, analyzing media and internet companies, and earning big money for a top bank. Then there was the moment when a new junior analyst was being given her very first city bonus.

That year we actually had an excellent year for the bank, and I'd given out the bonuses for each of my team, and they were, generally, very happy. However, when I handed out the bonus for my new junior analyst, a lovely big bonus, she left the room in tears. Everyone was shocked, even my own boss. After a bit of time for the dust to settle, I had a chance to ask her why she was so upset. She said she thought this was such a low bonus compared with her peers; she had worked hard and expected more.

Why am I writing about this? Well, it can be exactly the same thing in songwriting. Sometimes things don't work out. Sometimes we write an awesome song, but it never gets cut. Sometimes we work so hard for a particular cut, and it never gets heard in a pitch meeting with an artist, manager, or producer. In fact, that happens all the time.

The fact is, as often as not, it's not about our songs, the quality of our own work, or whether or not it 'deserves' being cut, but a totally random reason our song has been bumped for another song.

So what do we do when that happens? Shouldn't we feel unhappy? Yes, it's right to feel unhappy, especially when it's not fair or "right."

But, here's my suggestion: celebrate.

Celebrate the close shaves.

You are invited

IT'S TIME TO
CELEBRATE

A MISSED CUT SONG
HEY, BUT HERE'S TO NEXT TIME!

23 OCTOBER • 18:30
THE YACHT CLUB
BE THERE

Feeling unhappy should not stop us from writing another song that's even better. Even having the chance to get a cut and it doesn't work out, it's a disappointment, but it still means we are closer than we were before on our journey as a songwriter. And even though it may be difficult to see it this way at the time, a missed cut celebration is still worth having, along with an extra glass of wine to celebrate. Yes, I do that. And I know I'm not the only songwriter who does.

THE SONG FUNNEL

If you find you're putting in your best work and still not getting songs cut, here's something that might help. In business, there's a thing called the "sales funnel." This is a representation of how individual sales go through several stages, with fewer and fewer sales making it from one stage to the next: awareness, interaction, interest, and action (which ideally would be a sale).

As a songwriter, I have my own version: a Song Funnel. This similarly takes many ideas through their own journey through various stages: idea, writable, written, delivered through demos, cuts, and full recognition (just like the Song Chain). In reality, no matter how good your songs may be, there are always way more ideas than final songs that get recognized. I don't know what the percentage is from idea to recognition, but it's a very low percentage, even for a professional songwriter.

Here's a picture of what the Funnel looks like:

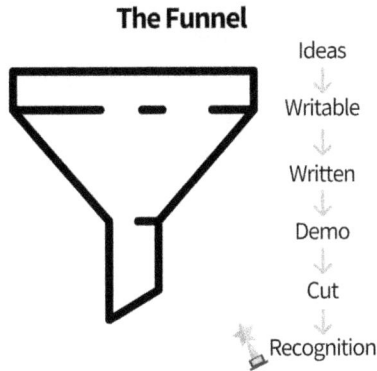

The Funnel

Ideas
↓
Writable
↓
Written
↓
Demo
↓
Cut
↓
Recognition

What this Funnel looks like is different for each songwriter (depending on their own journey and definition of success), but the trick of the Song Funnel, like the sales funnel, is to process as many ideas as possible. Many pro songwriters actively manage this process, whether they call it a funnel or not.

Why do so many songs not get cut?

Looking at the Funnel and the Song Chain in Part 2 of this book, it quickly becomes clear that most of us have very little control over what happens to our songs. For most of my time as a commercial songwriter, I've had very little control once a song was given to my publisher. Apart from doing everything I could to make it the best song possible, making use of my publisher's feedback to make it even better, there was very little I could do to help get it cut. Some of my best songs still are just not cut, and there are a million reasons why:

- Supply and demand — it's not that my songs are not great; it's just they're not needed right now
- Artist writing their own material

- Other writers pitching their songs harder or better
- Geography, timing, and personalities
- The number of publishers pitching other songs

Whatever the reasons a great song doesn't get cut, the big question is: what does that mean for us and our own why? The fact that your great songs don't get cut doesn't mean you're not a great writer, and it doesn't mean you should not be writing. Cuts are not the measure of your writing; that's mostly the measure of other people involved in the financial value part of the Song Chain after you send your songs into the world.

So what should you do if they are not cut? As I see it, there are three things you can do:

- Write another great song.
- Every now and again, review your catalog and enjoy the songs you've written.
- Think about whether there could be any new opportunities for your songs.

Enjoying the journey is the best reason to write more songs. The journey matters more than the destination anyway.

ONE LIFE, ONE CHANCE

OK, this is a philosophy rather than songwriting. But it's still worth asking the question:

> Where should I be spending my energy, time, and resources?

A while back, I had a health thing that made me ask this. And for the first time in my life, it made me realize that we really do only have one life, one chance on this planet. I don't have an answer for you about your own situation, but it's worth asking yourself now and again. For example, here are a few questions I've been asking myself:

- What's the right balance between craft and technology?
- Am I spending too much time and money on the studio?
- Should I spend more time in the Bible rather than looking for a song about it?
- Do I have a good balance between family and music? Music and writing?
- Should I look after my health more than my studio?

As I say, I have no answers for you; these are just questions. Don't forget to ask yourself big questions like this from time to time, too.

The Circle of Life

Here's something I've used for many years: the Circle of Life. You may well have seen it and used something like it already. This is what my circle looks like:

Circle of Life

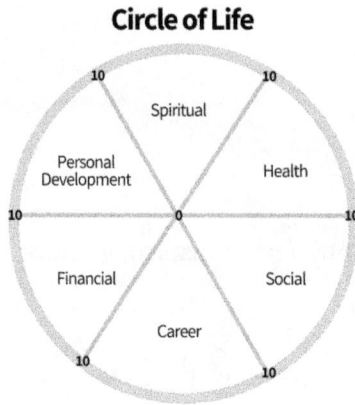

How does it work? It's simple.

For each segment of the circle, whether it's good or bad, simply give it a score out of 10, with a higher score representing how well things are going for you in that area of your life right now. It could be a one or a ten or somewhere in between. Sure, it's subjective. But you don't need to tell anyone what marks have been given to each segment; it's purely something for you and you alone.

Then, when you've marked all of these segments, simply join them all together and, hey presto, you have a picture of how bumpy life is right now — that's your Circle of Life. And it should show you which part of life probably needs some work.

As a songwriter, this has been incredibly helpful to do this now and again. It especially helps me realize if I'm spending too much time in Career (which is where Craft, Network, and Tech all sit), which might tell me that I need to spend a little less time with that and more with my family (Social) or with God (Spiritual).

Of course, this is not strictly about songwriting. But it might help you find out where songwriting should sit within the context of the rest of your life.

GOALS

If you didn't catch it, in front of each part of this book, I've given my own personal goals for each area. Just to summarize:

1. **Mindset** — To be the best version of a songwriter I can be.
2. **Ideas** — To have everything, everywhere.
3. **Tools** — To be a creative and prolific songwriter, even when I don't feel like it.
4. **Co-writing** — To best serve my co-writers, so we write the best song.
5. **Next Steps** — To focus on the journey, not just on the destination.

None of these goals are written in stone — your goals are likely different, and you may have more or fewer than five goals for your songwriting journey. But the point is: goals are helpful. They guide us in getting better at our craft, with our tools, and with our co-writers. Ultimately, having goals helps us enjoy our journey more. That's the only reason for having them.

Of all the advice and information in this book, the one statement I really want you to walk away with was on the very first page of this book, the first words of the Introduction:

Nothing is undoable. Just things not done.

What I mean is that whatever stage of your amazing songwriting journey you are at, you will probably see another hill or mountain you need to climb. When you do, just enjoy it. Because waiting to enjoy it until the end of your journey — your destination, wherever that is — is unlikely to be as much fun as the journey itself. Nothing is undoable on your journey.

- If you've not yet become the songwriter you want to be — it's not about things you can't do, it's just about things not yet done.
- If you haven't got all of your ideas and writable ideas with you everywhere — it's just about things not yet done.
- If you are not as creative and prolific a writer as you think you should be — it's just about things not yet done.
- If your co-writes are not yet focused on writing great songs together — it's just about things not yet done.
- Finally, if you are not focusing on the journey, just the destination — well, guess what? It's just about things not yet done.

My aim with this book is to give you the know-how and tools to get these things. I hope and pray this will be something you'll enjoy doing as much as I am.

SUMMARY

In the final few chapters of this book, I talked about how to organize the next steps on our own journey as songwriters, including what success really means to us. I also talked about the Song Funnel, and how important it is to get the right balance between our work as songwriters and the rest of life. These have all been key ideas for me as a songwriter.

So, as we come to a close, there are a couple of things I just wanted to say to you for reading this right to the end, as a kind of outro. Keep going!

Exercise

If you have a copy of *The Organized Songwriter Workbook*, this would be an excellent time to see Exercise 15.

OUTRO

In this book, I've tried to pass on everything I know about how to be organized as a songwriter, having taken the best left-brained logical approach to this right-brained creative, beautiful craft of songwriting. I hope and pray that this has been as useful to you as it has been for me.

As this final chapter draws to an end, I'd like to leave you with two thoughts. Firstly, thank you again for giving me your time. If you have read this book and completed all the exercises in the Workbook,

Congratulations! You are an Organized Songwriter!

YOU ARE AMAZING!

But whether you've gone through every part or chapter of this book, or even just dipped into the material in this book, my hope and prayer are for your songs to be powerful, beautiful, and emotionally charged.

Second, I would love to hear about your successes with the ideas, tools, and co-writing approaches you have learned about in this book.

If you meet me at a seminar or conference, please say hi to me! If you happen to be in one of my open critique sessions, warn me if your song will hit me with the songwriter's second secret weapon — that will make me jump up and down with joy!

But seriously, if this book has been helpful, I would love to hear from you, so please email me at:

simon@simonhawkins.com

May God bless you, your writing, and the extraordinary journey you have ahead of you.

– SJLH.

PART SIX

APPENDICES

APPENDIX A — TOP-25 WAYS TO FIND NEW TITLES

Here's a list of my favorite top-25 techniques to find new song titles (alphabetically):

1. Adage titles
2. Alliteration titles
3. Altering the adage titles
4. Antonym titles
5. Cause & effect titles
6. Colloquialism titles
7. Color titles
8. Conversation titles
9. Date titles
10. Epigram titles
11. Evolving situation titles
12. Literal & figurative titles
13. Maxim titles
14. Multi-character titles
15. Multi-meaning titles
16. Multi-time frame titles

17. Neutralized chorus titles
18. One-word titles
19. Physical & emotional titles
20. Place titles
21. Realization titles
22. Situation & reason titles
23. Time titles
24. Verse-show chorus-tells titles
25. Word-switch titles

APPENDIX B — TOP AWARDS FOR SONGWRITERS

Awards for songwriters:

- The American Music Awards (AMAs) for various genres. Created by Dick Clark Productions, the first of the three major music awards each year.
- The GRAMMY Awards for multiple genres and categories, presented by the Recording Academy.
- The Billboard Music Awards are given out annually by Billboard, with even more categories of genres.
- The Dove Awards for various Christian genres, presented by the Gospel Music Association (GMA).
- The Singing News Fan Awards, presented at the National Quartet Convention.
- The BRIT Awards, presented each year by the British Phonographic Industry (BPI) for pop music.
- The MOBO Awards (Music of Black Origin) are annually for music for "music of black origin," including hip-hop, grime, R&B, soul, reggae, jazz, gospel, and African music.
- The Mercury Prize is an annual music prize awarded for

the best album released in the United Kingdom by a British or Irish act. Established by the British Phonographic Industry (BPI) and the British Association of Record Dealers.

- The Ivors Academy Awards is presented annually in London by the British Academy of Songwriters, Composers and Authors (BASCA). Sponsored by the PRS, which is the main PRO in the UK.
- Various performance rights organizations (PROs) present their own awards at various times throughout the year, including ASCAP, BMI, SESAC, and SoundExchange in the US, and SOCAN, CMRRA, and Re:Sound in Canada.

Other major awards for songwriters and composers:

- The Academy Awards (Oscars), given by the Academy of Motion Picture Arts and Sciences (AMPAS) annually in February.
- The Golden Globe Awards are given out by 93 members of the Hollywood Foreign Press Association and presented each year in January.
- The Tony Awards (The Antoinette Perry Award for Excellence in Broadway Theatre) is held in June annually in NYC.

APPENDIX C — TOP-20 DOS AND DON'TS FOR CO-WRITING

This is all about etiquette. But what does that mean in terms of what should be done or not done in a co-writer. Here are my top-20 dos and don'ts:

DO

1. **DO bring writable ideas** — Especially if you are writing up, you will be asked to come up with a great idea. Bring them with you!
2. **DO be flexible** — Whatever is going to make a better song, do what needs to be done. Many jobs need to be done in the writing room, so choose a job the others are less strong at doing.
3. **DO tell them you're a fan** — Encouragement brings better-quality ideas when your co-writer knows they're performing for a supportive audience. Make your co-writer feel good about their input.
4. **DO say it, even if it sounds stupid** — Co-writers

love other writers who have the guts to say something odd or different, even if they sound dumb. It might point everyone on the way to a golden idea later.

5. **DO get the basics right** — Arrive early at the right place with the right people, great coffee, and a great writable idea. Boom. Take your diary, too, because you might pick a date for the next co-write.

6. **DO keep it in the room** — If your co-writer is talking confidential stuff, then keep it in the room. Most chit-chat is going to be confidential.

7. **DO keep going until it's right** — Keep working at the lyric and the melody until it's a great song, according to everyone. There's no CEO in a co-write.

8. **DO agree on shares upfront** — Get the royalty share money thing out of the way right upfront. Ideally, settle on equal equity shares. No one loves a word counter.

9. **DO take a break** — The best ideas often turn up at the most awkward moments (the loo). So make that moment happen.

10. **DO be fun** — Good hangs are generally asked to write again next time.

DON'T

1. **DON'T be negative** — Don't give negative comments about your co-writer's idea, even if you think it sucks. Find a way to positively say the same thing. Words like "Maybe," "What about," and "Let's pencil that in" are great phrases in a co-write.

2. **DON'T bring problems into the room** — Unless it's a song about your problem, leave it outside the room. Chances are they have more significant problems they could bring to a co-write, if that's the game you want to play.

3. **DON'T give up on your own craft** — Whatever part of the craft your co-writer is doing, keep coming up with alternative ideas because they might be the best ideas for the song. The idea fruit can be picked from the tree by anyone in the room.

4. **DON'T talk theory, write** — Sure, everyone likes talking about how beautiful the craft of songwriting is, but we're actually here to write a great song...so can we, er, maybe, er, start?

5. **DON'T steal others' ideas** — Your co-writers need to know that they can share their best ideas with you without you using it in your next co-write with someone else. Just be a good person.

6. **DON'T finish until it's finished** — A co-write isn't finished until the song is honestly finished. Sometimes it takes a lot longer than any wanted it to take. But it still needs to be finished.

7. **DON'T leave the room without a work tape** — It's always a mistake to finish without capturing the song in a recording. Better ideas could come later, but you need to know what initial ideas were captured first.

8. **DON'T oversell your ideas** — Sure, you need to pitch the idea enough for your co-writer to understand what it's about, but if they're not into your idea, just keep it for your next co-write.

9. **DON'T talk too much** — You need to hear your co-writer's thoughts, too. After all, they could be thinking better thoughts than yours!

10. **DON'T let your nerves kill the song** — Sure, everyone is nervous in the first three minutes, and that's what the first three minutes are for. Keep your eye on the nerve-free 177 minutes, which will be all about writing a great song (I've been there and still regret it).

APPENDIX D — TOP-20 KEY QUESTIONS

Here are my top-20 questions to answer as an **Organized Songwriter**.

Mindset

- What is your 'why' for songwriting?
- What is the passion behind your own songwriting
- What further competencies can you develop?
- Right now, how much do you spend on songwriting?

Ideas and Songs

- Are your song ideas and finished songs organized?
- What would help you create your own sacred space? And what should your space look like?
- What time of the day are you most creative? What time of the day is more creative for your co-writer (s)?
- What resources can you give to songwriting in terms of time? What about money? Assets?

Tools of the Trade

- What tools do you consider essential and which tools are nice to have for your craft?
- What other technology do you need to best support your craft?
- What networks do you not yet have? How will you access new networks?
- Where should I be spending my energy, time, and resources?

Co-writing

- How would you like your co-writer to serve you best?
- How do you think you can best prepare yourself for your next co-writer, mentally, physically, and even spiritually?
- Have you got all the details you need - the who, when, where, how long will it take to travel there? And, is it a FIRM date? Or is it a POSSIBLE co-write?
- How could you make your co-writer feel well-served?

Next steps

- What is your goal as a songwriter?
- What exactly does success look like?
- How critical is commercial success to you?
- What key milestones could make you feel you are moving forward with your songwriting journey?

APPENDIX E — TOP-20 ESSENTIAL TOOLS

I thought you might like to see my current top-20 list of tools I use as a songwriter. My Top-20 Essential Tools of the Trade for Songwriting in three categories:

1. Craft
2. Network
3. Technology

Craft

1. Sacred space

- My studio (right-brain place), with a long studio desk, two large screens, and a MacBook Pro.
- My office (left-brain place), with a separate, smaller desk and just one screen linked to a MacBook Air.
- The cool thing about the two laptops means my two sacred spaces can go with me anywhere mobile, especially in

Nashville. iPads are getting better and better, but are still not there yet for my use.

2. Sacred moment

- I'm grateful for being able to have sacred moments most days, even on weekends. Mornings are my most productive time. Afternoons are great for chilling, learning, and finishing things if I need to. Evenings are generally family time. That's important, too.

3. Creative habits

- Daily writing, freewriting, 15 minutes or 500 words most days
- Music writing, free playing, 15 minutes most days

4. All-weather writing

- Writing is something I love doing every day, whether writing songs or books. My former corporate career got me into the habit of working 9–10 hours a day if I need to. These days I try to have three meals with the family, which helps break up my work well.
- I'm using Scrivener, Notion, and Evernote for writing. I jump into FileMaker for several apps I've made myself. Really helpful.

5. Education

- Right now, I'm doing a Master's in Composing for Film, TV, and Games at Thinkspace/Chichester University.
- I love dipping into other courses at Berklee Music School, too.

- I love my work when I can move from writing songs and books to composing, worship, and demoing in the studio whenever I can.
- Jumping from left- to right-brain in one day is the best approach for me.

Network

6. Supportive family

- They keep me going, especially when I have the space to support them in their own lives, too.

7. Co-writers

- I wish I could write more with my list of co-writers. Video is fine, but I much prefer being with real people. Obviously, this is tricky, given social distancing.

8. Creative friends

- Zooming, Facebook, and FaceTime are the best ways for me to keep in touch right now. I've several new projects I'm thinking about doing when this book is finished.

9. Publisher

- I'm my own publisher (Great British Music Publishing) and, right now, I'm grateful to have this flexibility.

10. Critics

- Can critics really be a tool of the trade? Yes. Whenever I write a song it sooner or later needs to be listened to by someone, otherwise, what's the point of having it. I have a number of people I know will give me quality feedback on my songs, whether they are another publisher, a vicar or pastor at my church or even someone in my family I know will give me a critique on it. It's about trust and honesty.

Technology

11. Computer power

- My MacBook Pro laptop, for writing and as the heart of the studio.

12. Instruments

- Yamaha C3S Grand Piano, linked into the studio as a midi keyboard; various guitars including McPherson, Larrivée, and Fender Strat.

13. Remote controller

- My iPad Pro for Logic Remote with the piano. Incredibly helpful.

14. Software

- The studio has lots of plugins and VSTis. My top 5: Native-Instruments, Spitfire, Waves, Slate, and Output.

15. Hardware

- I've settled on three brands that have worked well for several years now: Genelec 8010A monitors with a 7060 Active Subwoofer, Prism Sound Orpheus ADA converters interface, and Neumann mics (U87, KMS 105, and town KM104). Great stuff.

16. To-do app

- Things 3, because I love the simplicity of it.

17. Lyric writing

- Google Docs and Word, capturing notes on Evernote and Apple Notes.

18. My Idea Bank

- On FileMaker Pro but I recently moved it onto Notion because it's so powerful.

19. DAW

- Logic Pro X 10.5 and Cubase 10.5.

20. Finally

- Of course, my iPhone, which I use all the time every day.

APPENDIX F — RESOURCES

One of the primary motivations for writing this book was to share ideas that are not found in any other publications. These ideas, tools, and co-writing material is such powerful stuff that I would love people to know about it, so please do pass on the information in this book to others you think will benefit.

There are other exceptional resources out there I would recommend if you have not yet found them, such as:

Books

- *Song Maps – A New System to Write Your Best Lyrics* and Audiobook by Simon Hawkins
- *Song Maps Workbook* by Simon Hawkins
- *The Organized Songwriter Workbook* by Simon Hawkins
- *Writing Better Lyrics* by Pat Pattison
- *Songwriting Without Boundaries* by Pat Pattison
- *Popular Lyric Writing* by Andrea Stolpe
- *Beginning Songwriting* by Andrea and Jan Stolpe
- *The Songwriter's Idea Book* by Sheila Davis

- *Successful Lyric Writing* by Sheila Davis
- *The Frustrated Songwriter's Handbook* by Karl Coryat
- *Songwriter's Journal* by Elizabeth Evans

Courses

- SongU.com
- Berklee Music School's Online Programs — particularly: Lyric Writing: Tools and Strategies, Lyric Writing: Writing Lyrics to Music, Lyric Writing: Writing From the Title, and Commercial Songwriting Techniques
- Kingdom Songs University - https://www. kingdomsongsuniversity.com/

Seminars

- Write About Jesus (WAJ) - www.writeaboutjesus.com

Support

- Nashville Songwriters Association International (NSAI) - https://www.nashvillesongwriters.com/
- Nashville Christian Songwriters (NCS) - https://www. nashvillechristiansongwriters.com/
- TAXI - https://www.taxi.com/

Apps:

- Songspace - https://songspace.com/
- Rhymer's Block - https://appsite. skygear.io/rhymer_s_block/
- Word Palette - http://www.wordpalette.io

NOTES

Are You Left or Right-Brained?

1. Although this book is not available on Kindle, it's highly recommended for our purposes. Other books by Sheila Davis are also well worth reading, including *The Songwriter's Idea Book* and *The Craft of Lyric Writing*.

What Does a Professional Songwriter Do?

1. Young Accountant of the Year (Global) while at Shell International, #1 Extel Analyst while at UBS, IR Society Awards for Reporting Annual Report while back in energy.

The Song Chain

1. See Appendix A to see a list of my top-25 ways to find new titles for your song
2. See Appendix B for more details of the main music awards.

1. Captured

1. Song titles are not copyrighted, so whatever songs you find, you can write that title in your own way, as evidenced in the approximately three million songs named "Fire," all of them excellent!

2. Writable

1. See *Song Maps - A New System to Write Your Best Lyrics*, Chapter 3 to find the important technical difference between plot and story.

4. Written

1. When two co-writers write a song, the equity share of each co-writer is normally 50%. With three co-writers, it's normally 33%, etc. I'd suggest being upfront about this in a new co-write because it's often difficult to feel totally creative if you're worried about what the deal is.

The Songwriter's Secret Weapons II

1. If you can find a Song Map for Queen's "Bohemian Rhapsody," I'd honestly love to hear from you at simon@simonhawkins.com!

Your Best Investment

1. The GMA now holds this event under the name "Immerse" here: https://www.experienceimmerse.com

5. Education

1. Thinkspace Education is a brilliant global resource for upcoming composers and sound designers. I'm still working on my Masters in Composing for Film, TV, and Games. https://thinkspaceeducation.com
2. The Rabbit Room is a wonderful community involved in music, story, and art founded by Pete and Andrew Peterson https://rabbitroom.com/

1. Being in the Right Place

1. See Appendix C for a list of suggested dos and don'ts for songwriting.

THANK YOUS

I wish I could mention everyone who has helped me on my journey writing this book, but there simply isn't space. Without a doubt, my incredibly supportive family in England and my 100 wonderful co-writers from all over the world deserve to be listed here.

Special thanks to my wife Sandra, who has not just given me all the space to write songs but has also given me the time to write this second book. Here's to the third!

Thanks to my children, Poppy, Monty, and Barty. They are an inspiration in so many ways.

To my second editor, Molly Hawkins (my Mum!), who had edited this book twice and still found my mistakes. She's amazing! I know my late father, Norman Hawkins, would be proud of her as well as for this book.

Thanks to Sue C Smith and Holly Ward for signing me to my first staff publishing deal in Nashville at Brentwood-Benson Music Publishing (now Universal/Capitol CMG Publishing). I am still so grateful to you.

Thanks also to my wonderful co-writers and extended family in Nashville and at WAJ, who were guinea pigs for much of the material presented in this book in my Getting Organized class. You have given back so much more than you know.

Thanks to Pat Pattison and Andrea Stolpe at Berklee Music School, without whom I would never have gotten signed as a staff songwriter in the first place.

Special thanks to my editor, Harry Althoff - this dude has made this book so much better than I imagined. Thank you, Harry! And thanks to Sven Sjöberg, my designer.

Special thanks to Dr. Lloyd Bradley and Sarah Johnson at the Donald Wilson Neurological Rehab Centre at St. Richard's Hospital, Chichester, who got me writing again when all the words were gone.

Thank you. You are all genuinely awesome people to work with.

ABOUT THE AUTHOR

Simon Hawkins is an award-winning songwriter, producer, and Amazon best-selling author, based on the south coast of England.

In 2004, Simon became a full-time songwriter and was quickly signed by Universal Music Publishing in Nashville (Brentwood-Benson Music Publishing/Universal CMG), where he has some 200 songs in his catalog. In 2010, he founded his publishing company, Great British Music, which now represents his work.

Simon's songs have been recorded by Vince Gill and Sheri Easter ("Livin' in the Rain"), American Idol finalist Mandisa ("Truth About Me"), Abandon ("Known"), Avalon ("Destined"), Gold City ("Never Too Broken") and many others in a range of genres.

"Livin' in the Rain" reached #2 on the SoGo charts and was long-listed for a Grammy. In 2012, Mandisa's album "What If We Were Real," which included "Truth About Me," was nominated for a Grammy. "Never Too Broken" reached #1 on the SoGo charts in autumn 2014. Simon also received a Dove nomination for the musical LifeSong: The Musical, written with Sue C Smith.

In 2015, Simon's modern hymn "He Is God" won the Integrity Music "Search for a Hymn 2015" competition, which he recorded with Integrity/Thankyou Music.

Simon's book *Song Maps - A New System to Write Your Best Lyrics* is still a #1 best seller on Amazon, internationally.

Simon is on the faculty of Write About Jesus, an annual conference based in St Louis, Missouri, that aims to equip and inspire Christian songwriters. He is also part of Harbour Creative, an HTB church plant in Portsmouth, England.

facebook.com/sjlhawkins

twitter.com/sjlhawkins

instagram.com/sjlhawkins

ALSO BY SIMON HAWKINS

The Organized Songwriter — How to Create Space to Write Your Best
Songs

The Organized Songwriter Workbook

———

Song Maps — A New System to Write Your Best Lyrics

Song Maps Workbook

*** HELP! ***

Thank you for reading this book

I really appreciate all of your feedback, and I love hearing what you have to say

Please leave me a helpful REVIEW

Thank you so much!

Enjoy being an Organized Songwriter!

www.ingramcontent.com/pod-product-compliance
Lightning Source LLC
Chambersburg PA
CBHW051904090426
42811CB00003B/462